The Ultimate Ninja Speedi

Cookbook for Beginners

The Simple & Selected Ninja Speedi Recipes Will Help

You Make the Best Tasting Fried Food

Miyoko Delvalle

CONTENTS

Introduction

The Ninja Speedi is a fantastic kitchen appliance that offers many cooking options. With its unique combination of air frying, steaming, and both functions, you can create tasty and nutritious meals that cook simultaneously on two levels. It also comes with a range of settings, including Steam & Crisp, Slow Cook, and Sous Vide, giving you even more flexibility in your cooking.

The Speedi is designed for ultimate convenience, with a lever on the lid allowing you to switch between Air Fry and Rapid Cooker modes easily. The touchscreen control panel gives you access to all 12 functions, making it super easy to operate. Whether a beginner or an experienced cook, the Ninja Speedi is simple to use and helps you cook confidently like a pro chef.

The Speedi air fryer is a must-have appliance for any kitchen. It is designed to fit easily under a cabinet with the lid down, but when used, it should be pulled out onto the countertop to provide enough space to raise the lid. This intuitive appliance has a large removable cooking pot and a crisper tray. The comprehensive manual and additional resources provide helpful tips and instructions to get you started.

For a hassle-free cooking experience, the Speedi Meal Builder offers a range of suggested food combinations and cooking times. This feature is handy if you're unsure what to cook or want to try something new. The accompanying pamphlet and booklet also provide instructions on how to make Speedi Meals, recipes, and cooking charts. Professional chefs and home cooks can benefit from the convenience and versatility of the Speedi, making it an excellent choice for anyone looking for an efficient and stress-free cooking experience.

Fundamentals of Ninja Speedi

The Ninja Speedi is an incredible kitchen gadget that provides many cooking options. Its distinctive blend of air frying, steaming, and both features allows you to whip up delicious and healthy meals that cook on two levels simultaneously. Moreover, it comes with various settings, such as Steam & Crisp, Slow Cook, and Sous Vide, providing even more versatility in your cooking.

What is Ninja Speedi ?

The Speedi air fryer is the ultimate kitchen companion for any household. It's designed to fit easily under a cabinet with the lid down, but when in use, it needs to be pulled forward on the countertop to ensure enough space to raise the lid. The Speedi has features, including a large removable cooking pot and a flat crisper tray, making it an excellent choice for cooking all sorts of dishes.

The Speedi manual and pamphlet provide clear instructions on preparing Speedi Meals and a booklet of mouth-watering recipes, colorful photos, and helpful cooking charts. Additionally, you can access the Speedi Meal Builder online, which suggests various food combinations and cooking times. With the Speedi, you can easily create professional dishes in your kitchen.

Benefits of Using It

The Speedi Meals function lets you quickly and easily make a delicious meal for up to four people in just 15 minutes.

With a 6-quart capacity, you can create a wholesome one-pot meal with your choice of base, vegetables, and protein to satisfy the whole family. The Speedi Meals function takes the guesswork out of meal planning so you can enjoy your meal quickly.

Our 12-in-1 functionality gives you maximum cooking flexibility. Rapid Cooker mode unlocks Speedi Meals, Steam

& Crisp, Steam & Bake, Steam, and Proof options. Switch to Air Fry mode and discover new culinary possibilities - including Air Fry, Bake/Roast, Broil, Dehydrate, Sear & Sauté, Slow Cook, and Sous Vide functions. With this professional-grade appliance, you'll have the power to make all your favorite dishes easily.

The Rapid Cooking System of the Speedi appliance allows you to create steam, caramelize, and air fry food simultaneously in one pot, resulting in restaurant-quality dishes. Take advantage of the Rapid Cooker mode and enjoy professional-level meals at home.

Experience the ultimate cooking convenience with SmartSwitch functionality, which allows you to easily switch between Air Fry mode and Rapid Cooker mode, opening up a world of delicious possibilities. With this professional-grade feature, you can quickly master any dish and add an extra kick of flavor to your meals. Start enjoying the convenience of SmartSwitch today and unleash your kitchen's full potential!

The Ninja Speedi Meal Builder unlocks thousands of customizable recipes tailored to the ingredients in your fridge or pantry. This easy-to-use tool helps you create the perfect dish quickly and professionally. So why wait? Start building your Speedi Meal today!

Air frying is a healthier way to prepare meals, with up to 75% less fat than traditional deep frying. We've tested it

against hand-cut, deep-fried French fries, and the results speak for themselves. Enjoy the same delicious taste without the guilt - air fry your meals today and start eating healthier!

Speedi Cleanup offers a fast and easy solution to your cleanup needs. Our nonstick pot and crisper tray are dishwasher-safe, making cleaning a breeze. With this professional-grade kitchenware, you can enjoy quick and efficient cleaning in no time.

Main functions of Ninja Speedi

The Ninja Speedi is a groundbreaking appliance that offers 12 special cooking functions, providing optimal conditions for preparing delicious meals with precision.

1. SPEEDI MEALS:

This versatile appliance allows you to create two-part meals quickly with just one touch. Whether you're a seasoned chef or a home cook, you'll love how easy it is to create mouth-watering meals with the Speedi Meals function. No more guesswork in meal planning! With the Ninja Speedi, you can enjoy delicious, nutritious meals perfect for your busy lifestyle. And the best part? You won't have to compromise on taste or quality. So why wait? Try the Ninja Speedi today and savor every delectable bite!

2. STEAM & CRISP:

Experience the ultimate blend of juicy and crispy results with the perfect balance of moisture and crunch, thanks to the Steam & Crisp function. This innovative feature is designed to cater to professional chefs and home cooks, offering the convenience and ease of use needed to prepare perfectly cooked food every time. Enjoy healthier meals with reduced fat and calories while savoring your favorite dishes' satisfying texture and flavor. Trust in the Steam & Crisp function to create mouth-watering meals you feel good about.

3. STEAM & CRISP BAKE:

Experience a new level of precision and control in baking with the STEAM & CRISP BAKE Function of the Ninja Speedi. You can now bake fluffier cakes and quick bread in less time and with less fat. This professional-grade baking solution is always designed to provide perfect results, allowing you to enjoy light, fluffy cakes and bread. With the Ninja Speedi, you can now easily create healthier and delicious baked goods.

4. STEAM:

The Ninja Speedi's Steam mode is perfect for gently cooking delicate foods at a high temperature. With this professional-grade cooking feature, you can enjoy perfectly cooked dishes with minimal effort. Trust in the advanced technology of the Ninja Speedi to cook your meals precisely as you intended every time.

5. PROOF:

The Ninja Speedi is a must-have appliance for professional bakers who want to craft the perfect dough for their delicious creations. Its advanced temperature and humidity controls provide the perfect environment for the dough to rest and rise, allowing bakers to create consistent and incredible results every time. With Ninja Speedi, you can be confident in your baking and enjoy delicious, perfectly risen dough for all your baked goods.

6. Air Fry:

Enjoy your favorite fried foods guilt-free with the AIR FRY Function of the Ninja Speedi. This function lets you fry your favorite foods with minimal oil, so you can indulge without worrying about extra calories. Whether you're craving crispy French fries or perfectly fried chicken, the AIR FRY Function provides a healthier alternative to traditional deep frying. So go ahead, and indulge in your favorite fried foods while still maintaining a healthy and fit lifestyle.

7. BAKE/ROAST

Looking to quickly and easily roast meats, vegetables, and more? The Bake/Roast function on the Ninja Speedi is the perfect solution. It transforms your appliance into an efficient roaster oven that maintains the flavor and texture of your food. Whether you're cooking for a large group or meal prepping for the week, Bake/Roast is the perfect solution. With this function, you can easily enjoy delicious, perfectly cooked baked treats and tender roasted meats in no time.

8. Broil:

Add texture, color, and crispness to your meals with the Ninja Speedi's Caramelize Function. This advanced cooking method allows you to create healthy, delectable, crispy and caramelized dishes. From melting cheese on burgers and pasta to caramelizing sugar on top of pudding and Brulee, this function offers endless possibilities to experiment with different recipes and enhance the flavor of your ingredients. With this innovative technique, you can make your meals healthier and tastier, unlocking a new level of culinary creativity.

9. DEHYDRATE:

Its advanced dehydrating function lets you enjoy the best dry food without expensive dehydrators. This function simplifies your kitchen setup by eliminating the need for overpriced and complicated dehydrators, making it an ideal choice for professionals and health-conscious individuals. Get ready to experience the convenience and high-quality results of Ninja Speedi for all your dehydrated food needs.

10. SOUS VIDE:

With sous vide, you have complete control over the temperature to achieve perfect results. High-end restaurants have used this cooking method for years to ensure that each dish is cooked to the ideal level of doneness. With the Ninja Speedi, you can now bring the same precision and quality to your home cooking, enjoying restaurant-quality meals every time.

11. SLOW COOK:

The Slow Cooker Mode of the Ninja Speedi is the ultimate solution for perfectly cooked meals without spending all day in the kitchen. This innovative mode lets you cook your food at a lower temperature for extended periods, freeing up your time for other activities. With the Ninja Speedi Slow Cooker Mode, you can enjoy delicious, high-quality meals without compromising your busy schedule.

12. SEAR/SAUTÉ:

With its professional stovetop tools, the Ninja Speedi now allows you to achieve restaurant-quality cooking in your own kitchen. You can easily create gourmet-level dishes quickly and precisely with the ability to brown meats, sauté vegetables, simmer sauces, and more. Enjoy the convenience and high-quality results of a professional stovetop right at home with your Ninja Speedi.

Step-By-Step Using Ninja Speedi

SPEEDI MEALS:

1. Make sure to remove the Crisper Tray from the bottom of the pot before starting.
2. Follow the recipe instructions to add the liquid and ingredients to the pot's bottom.
3. Extend the legs on the Crisper Tray, and put the tray in the raised position inside the pot. Then, add the ingredients to the tray as specified in the recipe.
4. Switch the SmartSwitch to the RAPID COOKER setting, and use the center arrows to select Speedi Meals. The default setting will show up on display. Adjust the temperature by using the up and down arrows to the left of the display in increments of 10 or 15 degrees from 250°F to 450°F.
5. Modify the cooking time by using the arrows on the right of the display, in 1-minute steps, up to a maximum of 30 minutes.
6. Press START/STOP to start cooking.
7. The progress bars on display will indicate that the unit is generating steam. Once the steam level reaches the appropriate

level, the timer will start counting down.

8. When the cooking time runs out, the unit will beep and display "End." If your food needs additional cooking time, use the up arrows on the right of the display to increase the cooking time.

STEAM & CRISP:

1. Collect all the ingredients specified in your recipe.

2. Set the SmartSwitch to the RAPID COOKER mode, and select Steam & Crisp using the center front arrows. The default setting will appear on display.

3. Adjust the temperature by using the up and down arrows to the left of the display in increments of 10 or 15 degrees between 250°F and 450°F.

4. Modify the cooking time by using the arrows to the right of the display, in 1-minute steps, up to a maximum of 30 minutes.

5. Press START/STOP to begin cooking. The progress bars on display will show that the unit is building steam.

6. The timer will start counting down once the unit reaches the proper steam level.

7. When the cooking time reaches zero, the unit will beep and display "End." If your food needs more cooking time, use the up arrow on the right of the display to add extra time. The unit will skip the preheating process.

STEAM & BAKE:

1. Start by placing the Crisper Tray at the bottom and the baking accessories on top of your RAPID COOKER.

2. Set the SmartSwitch to the RAPID COOKER mode, and use the center arrows to select STEAM & BAKE.

3. The default temperature setting will appear on display, and you can adjust it using the up and down arrows on the left in 10 or 15-degree increments between 250°F and 400°F.

4. To adjust the cooking time, use the up and down arrows on the right of the display to set a time between 1 minute and 1 hour and 15 minutes in 1-minute steps.

5. Press START/STOP when you're ready to start cooking. The progress bars on display will indicate the unit is building steam. The timer will begin counting down once preheating is finished.

6. When the cooking time expires, the unit will beep and display "End." If you need to cook the food further, press the up arrow on the right of the display to add extra time.

7. The unit will skip the preheating step for additional cooking.

STEAM:

1. Start by adding water to the bottom of the pot, and place the Crisper Tray in the bottom position. Then add your desired ingredients.

2. Set the SmartSwitch to the RAPID COOKER mode, and use the center front arrows to select STEAM.

3. Use the up and down arrows on the right of the display to adjust the cooking time.

4. Once you've set the cooking time, press START/STOP to begin cooking.

5. The unit will preheat to bring the liquid to a boil. The progress bars on display will indicate the unit is building steam. When the preheating is finished, the timer will start counting down. The preheating animation will appear on the display until the unit reaches temperature, and then switch to the timer counting down.

6. When the cooking time is up, the unit will beep and display "End." By following these steps, you can ensure a successful cooking experience

PROOF:

1. Place the Crisper Tray at the bottom of the pot and add dough to the baking accessory. Place the accessory on top of the tray.

2. Set the SmartSwitch to the RAPID COOKER setting, and use the center front arrows to select PROOF. The default temperature setting will display. Adjust the temperature from 90°F to 105°F in 5-degree increments using the up and

down arrows to the left of the display.

3. Adjust the proof time from 15 minutes to 4 hours in 5-minute increments using the up and down arrows to the right of the display.

4. Press START/STOP to start proofing.

5. When the proofing time reaches zero, the unit will beep and display "End." Follow these steps carefully for successful proofing.

SEAR/SAUTÉ:

1. To begin cooking, remove the Crisper Tray from the pot and add your ingredients.

2. Move the SmartSwitch to AIR FRY/STOVETOP and use the center front arrows to select the desired heat setting, ranging from "Lo1" to "Hi5".

3. Press START/STOP to start cooking, and the timer will begin counting up. To stop the SEAR/SAUTÉ function, press START/STOP. If you want to switch to a different cooking function, first press START/STOP to end the current function, and then use the SmartSwitch and center front arrows to choose your desired function.

SLOW COOK:

1. Remove the crisper tray before adding your ingredients to the slow cooker pot. Check the maximum fill line (indicated inside the pot) to avoid overfilling.

2. Move the SmartSwitch to AIR FRY/STOVETOP and select SLOW COOK using the center front arrows. The default temperature setting will appear on display. Use the up and down arrows to the left of the display to choose between "Hi," "Lo," or "BUFFET" settings.

3. Use the up and down arrows to the right of the display to adjust the cooking time. Press START/STOP to begin the cooking process.

4. When the cooking time is up, the unit will beep and automatically switch to Keep Warm mode while counting up.

SOUS VIDE:

1. Before starting the sous vide process, remove the crisper

tray from the pot and add 12 cups of room-temperature water to the marked level.

2. Close the lid and select AIR FRY/STOVETOP on the dial, then use the center arrows to choose SOUS VIDE. The default temperature setting will be displayed. Use the up and down arrows to the left of the display to set a temperature in 5-degree increments from 120°F to 190°F.

3. The default cook time is 3 hours, but you can adjust the time in 15-minute increments up to 12 hours, then in 1-hour increments up to 24 hours, using the up and down arrows on the right of the display.

4. Press START/STOP to begin preheating. The unit will beep when preheating is complete, and the display will show "ADD FOOD." To place the bags in the water, use the water displacement method: Leave a corner of the bag unzipped and slowly lower the bag into the water, allowing the water pressure to force the air out of the bag and causing it to submerge. Repeat for each bag.

Air Fry:

1. Prepare your cooking station by placing your Crisper Tray in the bottom position.

2. Next, add your desired ingredients to the pot and close the lid. Switch the SmartSwitch to AIR FRY/STOVETOP, and the unit will default to AIR FRY mode.

3. The default temperature will be displayed, but for precise cooking, use the up and down arrows on the left side of the display to choose a temperature between 250°F and 400°F in 10 or 15-degree increments.

4. Adjust the cooking time as needed using the up and down arrows on the right side of the display, with increments of 1 minute up to 1 hour.

5. Press START/STOP to begin cooking and let the unit work its magic.

6. When the cooking time reaches zero, the unit will beep and display "End," indicating that your meal is ready. Follow these professional and easy-to-follow instructions

for delicious results every time!

BAKE/ROAST

1. Before starting the cooking process, ensure that the Crisper Tray is placed at the bottom of the pot.

2. Move the SmartSwitch to AIR FRY/STOVETOP, and then use the center front arrows to select the BAKE/ROAST option.

3. The default temperature setting will be displayed. To achieve precise cooking, use the up and down arrows to the left of the display to choose a temperature between 300°F to 400°F with increments of either 10 or 15 degrees.

4. The up and down arrows to the right of the display can be used to set the cooking time up to 1 hour in 1-minute increments or from 1 hour to 4 hours in 5-minute increments.

5. Finally, press START/STOP to begin the cooking process. When the cooking time reaches zero, the unit will beep, and the display will show "End."

6. With these simple steps, you can achieve the perfect bake or roast every time.

Broil:

1. Place the ingredients on the Crisper Tray in an elevated position before closing the lid for optimal results.

2. Then, move the SmartSwitch to AIR FRY/STOVETOP and select BROIL using the center front arrows. The default temperature setting will be displayed, and you can set the temperature between 400°F to 450°F in 25-degree increments using the up and down arrows to the left of the display.

3. You can adjust the cooking time to 30 minutes in 1-minute increments using the up and down arrows to the right of the display. Press START/STOP to begin cooking.

4. The unit will beep and display "End" when the cooking time reaches zero. Follow these simple steps for perfectly broiled dishes every time.

DEHYDRATE:

1. Before starting your dehydrating session, place the Crisper Tray at the bottom of the pot.

2. Move the SmartSwitch to AIR FRY/STOVETOP and select DEHYDRATE with the center front arrows. The default temperature setting will be displayed. You can adjust the temperature between 105°F and 195°F by using the up and down arrows to the left of the display.

3. To adjust the cooking time, use the up and down arrows to the right of the display. You can set the cooking time between 1 and 12 hours in 15-minute increments.

4. Press START/STOP to begin the dehydrating process.

5. When the cooking time reaches zero, the unit will beep,

and the display will show "End" to indicate the end of the cooking session. Follow these steps for successful and efficient dehydration.

Tips for Using Accessories

Remove and dispose of all packaging materials, stickers, and tape before using your unit.

It is crucial to carefully read and follow the operational instructions, warnings, and necessary safeguards to ensure the safety of yourself and your property.

For optimal operation, wash the removable pot, crisper tray, and condensation collector in warm, soapy water, then rinse and dry them thoroughly.

Cleaning and Caring for Ninja Speedi

To ensure that your Ninja Speedi operates optimally, cleaning it thoroughly before and after each use is essential. Here are the steps to follow for proper cleaning:

Before beginning the cleaning process, disconnect the central unit from the power source.

Use a damp cloth to wipe down the main unit and control panel.

Dishwasher-safe accessories like the basket and crisper plate can be placed in the dishwasher.

Soak plates with tough food residues in warm soapy water to remove them.

Dry all parts with a towel or allow them to air dry.

Following these steps, you can ensure your Ninja Speedi is properly cleaned and ready to provide optimal performance.

Frequently Asked Questions & Notes

1. The Steam function on the unit generates significant amounts of steam.

Steam is released through the vent during cooking is a regular occurrence.

2. An error message reading "ADD POT" is displayed on the screen.

The unit displays an "ADD POT" error message when the complete meal pot is not placed inside the cooker base, as it is required for all functions.

4-Week Meal Plan

Week 1

Day 1:
Breakfast: Eggs & Ham Sandwiches
Lunch: Cauliflower with Onion
Snack: Cauliflower Rice
Dinner: Seasoned Turkey Breast
Dessert: Apple Pies

Day 2:
Breakfast: Cinnamon Toast
Lunch: Trimmed Yellow Beans with Tomatoes
Snack: Cheese Portobello Patties
Dinner: Chinese Stir-Fry Chicken
Dessert: Pecan-Stuffed Apples

Day 3:
Breakfast: Rainbow Bread Sticks
Lunch: Cremini Mushroom Slices
Snack: Chopped Cauliflower
Dinner: Coconut Steak
Dessert: Sweet 'n' Salty Granola Bark

Day 4:
Breakfast: Lox Avocado Toast
Lunch: Yukon Gold Potatoes
Snack: Cilantro Tofu Cubes
Dinner: Sea Bass Fillet with Tomato
Dessert: Chocolate Croissants

Day 5:
Breakfast: Egg "Quiche Lorraine" Cups
Lunch: Caponata with Twist
Snack: Brussels Sprouts
Dinner: Keto Chicken Breasts
Dessert: Chocolate Molten Cakes

Day 6:
Breakfast: Cheddar Tater Tot Egg Cups
Lunch: Cheese Broccoli Florets
Snack: Cheddar Zucchini Balls
Dinner: Beef Steak Strips
Dessert: Coconut Toast

Day 7:
Breakfast: Cheese Spinach Frittata
Lunch: Loaded Chickpea & Cauliflower Salad
Snack: Mustard Cauliflower & Broccoli
Dinner: Honey Garlic Trout
Dessert: Homemade Pumpkin Fritters

Week 2

Day 1:
Breakfast: Cheddar Ham Strata
Lunch: Greek Roasted Beets
Snack: Egg Mushroom Fritters
Dinner: Simple Chicken Thighs
Dessert: Chocolate-Frosted Doughnuts

Day 2:
Breakfast: Raisin Rice Cereal
Lunch: Mediterranean Green Beans
Snack: Keto Mushroom Risotto
Dinner: Minced Beef & Pepper Bowl
Dessert: Homemade Chocolate Chip Cookies

Day 3:
Breakfast: Hazelnut Chocolate Granola
Lunch: Chinese Brussels Sprouts
Snack: Cheddar Broccoli Tots
Dinner: Cauliflower Lamb Fritters
Dessert: Stuffed Baked Apples

Day 4:
Breakfast: Pecan Pumpkin Cereal
Lunch: Italian Eggplant Slices
Snack: Chives and Spinach Chops
Dinner: Classic Thanksgiving Turkey Breasts
Dessert: Apple Hand Pies

Day 5:
Breakfast: Mix Trail Oatmeal
Lunch: Flavorful Cauliflower Florets
Snack: Zucchini Tots
Dinner: Typical Chicken Legs
Dessert: Blueberry Pie

Day 6:
Breakfast: Loaded Quesadillas
Lunch: Steak Fries
Snack: Egg Broccoli Hash Brown
Dinner: Asian-Style Duck Breast
Dessert: Old-Fashioned Cherry Cobbler

Day 7:
Breakfast: Buttermilk Biscuits
Lunch: Fried Green Tomatoes
Snack: Eggplant Bites
Dinner: BBQ Beef Steaks
Dessert: Banana Cake

Week 3

Day 1:
Breakfast: Onion Corn Muffins
Lunch: Fried Okra with Lemon Wedges
Snack: Cream Broccoli Puree
Dinner: Tiger Prawns with Sherry Wine
Dessert: Chocolate Cake

Day 2:
Breakfast: Caramel Banana Muffins
Lunch: Hush Puppies
Snack: Seasoned Brussel Sprouts
Dinner: Carrot Chicken Salad
Dessert: Fudge Brownies

Day 3:
Breakfast: Blueberry Muffins with Lemon Zest
Lunch: Mexican Street Ears of Corn
Snack: Coriander Fennel Wedges
Dinner: Garlicky Beef Steak
Dessert: Almond Cake with Chopped Plums

Day 4:
Breakfast: Toffee Zucchini Bread
Lunch: Cherry Tomatoes with Basil
Snack: Turmeric Tempeh
Dinner: Black Cod with Grapes
Dessert: Cream Muffins

Day 5:
Breakfast: Nutty Squash Bread
Lunch: Turkish Leek Fritters
Snack: Cheese Banana Peppers Mix
Dinner: Paprika Chicken Cutlets
Dessert: Fried Plums

Day 6:
Breakfast: Eggs & Ham Sandwiches
Lunch: Caribbean Yuca Fries
Snack: Keto Cauliflower Chops
Dinner: Rib Eye Steaks
Dessert: Pecan-Stuffed Apples

Day 7:
Breakfast: Rainbow Bread Sticks
Lunch: Coated Shishito Pepper
Snack: Keto Cabbage Coleslaw
Dinner: Maple-Glazed Salmon
Dessert: Chocolate Croissants

Week 4

Day 1:
Breakfast: Cinnamon Toast
Lunch: Maple-Soy Brussels Sprouts
Snack: Brussel Sprouts with Coconut Shred
Dinner: Roll Chicken Sliders
Dessert: Coconut Toast

Day 2:
Breakfast: Egg "Quiche Lorraine" Cups
Lunch: Cauliflower with Onion
Snack: Cauliflower Rice
Dinner: Curry Beef Chops
Dessert: Chocolate Molten Cakes

Day 3:
Breakfast: Lox Avocado Toast
Lunch: Cremini Mushroom Slices
Snack: Cheese Portobello Patties
Dinner: Large Shrimp with Amaretto Glaze
Dessert: Stuffed Baked Apples

Day 4:
Breakfast: Cheddar Tater Tot Egg Cups
Lunch: Yukon Gold Potatoes
Snack: Cilantro Tofu Cubes
Dinner: Mexican-Style Chicken Taquitos
Dessert: Chocolate-Frosted Doughnuts

Day 5:
Breakfast: Cheddar Ham Strata
Lunch: Loaded Chickpea & Cauliflower Salad
Snack: Cheddar Zucchini Balls
Dinner: Jalapeno Beef Casserole
Dessert: Homemade Chocolate Chip Cookies

Day 6:
Breakfast: Cheese Spinach Frittata
Lunch: Greek Roasted Beets
Snack: Mustard Cauliflower & Broccoli
Dinner: Lime Duck Breast
Dessert: Apple Hand Pies

Day 7:
Breakfast: Raisin Rice Cereal
Lunch: Mediterranean Green Beans
Snack: Zucchini Tots
Dinner: Hawaiian Chicken Legs with Pineapple
Dessert: Blueberry Pie

Chapter 1 Breakfast Recipes

Eggs & Ham Sandwiches

Prep Time: 10 minutes | Cook Time: 6 minutes | Serves: 2

4 slices gluten-free sandwich bread

2 tablespoons butter, melted and divided

4 large eggs, scrambled

4 slices deli ham

2 slices Colby cheese

4 teaspoons basil pesto sauce

1. Brush two pieces gluten-free bread with half of butter. 2. Place the Crisper Tray in the bottom position. Add the bread to it and divide eggs, ham, and cheese on each bread slices; close the lid. Spread pesto on remaining bread slices and place slices pesto side down onto sandwiches in basket. Brush remaining butter on tops of sandwiches. 3. Move SmartSwitch to AIR FRY/STOVETOP, set the cooking temperature to 375°F and the cooking time to 6 minutes. Flip the food halfway through. 4. Serve warm.

Per Serving: Calories 660; Fat: 39.22g; Sodium: 1371mg; Carbs: 37.74g; Fiber: 6.1g; Sugar: 5.83g; Protein: 38.8g

Cinnamon Toast

Prep Time: 10 minutes | Cook Time: 8 minutes | Serves: 2

¼ cup granulated sugar

1½ teaspoons ground cinnamon

2 tablespoons butter, room temperature

4 slices gluten-free sandwich bread

1. Combine sugar and cinnamon in a small bowl. 2. Spread butter over bread slices and evenly sprinkle buttered slices with cinnamon-sugar mix. 3. Place the Crisper Tray in the bottom position. Add the bread slices to it and close the lid. Move SmartSwitch to AIR FRY/STOVETOP, set the cooking temperature to 375°F and the cooking time to 4 minutes. You can cook the bread slices in batches. 4. Serve warm.

Per Serving: Calories 373; Fat: 15.01g; Sodium: 404mg; Carbs: 49.59g; Fiber: 7.1g; Sugar: 17.52g; Protein: 11.15g

Rainbow Bread Sticks

Prep Time: 10 minutes | Cook Time: 10 minutes | Serves: 4

1 large egg

⅓ cup whole milk

⅛ teaspoon salt

½ teaspoon ground cinnamon

1 cup crushed Post Fruity Pebbles cereal

4 slices gluten-free sandwich bread, each cut into 4 sticks

¼ cup pure maple syrup

1. Whisk the egg, milk, salt and cinnamon in a small bowl. 2. Add cereal crumbs in a small dish. 3. Dip the bread stick in the egg mixture and then dredge in cereal crumbs. 4. Place the Crisper Tray in the bottom position. Add the bread sticks to it and close the lid. Move SmartSwitch to AIR FRY/STOVETOP, set the cooking temperature to 375°F and the cooking time to 5 minutes. 5. Flip the food after 3 minutes of cooking time. 6. Transfer sticks to a large plate and serve warm with maple syrup to dip.

Per Serving: Calories 235; Fat: 4.06g; Sodium: 313mg; Carbs: 41.69g; Fiber: 3.3g; Sugar: 20.27g; Protein: 8.27g

Lox Avocado Toast

Prep Time: 10 minutes | Cook Time: 10 minutes | Serves: 2

1 medium avocado, peeled and pitted

1 clove garlic, peeled and minced

¼ teaspoon lime juice

⅛ teaspoon salt

2 slices gluten-free bread

2 medium Campari tomatoes, sliced

¼ teaspoon ground black pepper

4 ounces smoked salmon

2 tablespoons capers

2 tablespoons diced peeled red onion

1. In a small bowl, Press avocado flesh, garlic, lime juice, and salt in a small bowl until desired consistency is reached. 2. Spread the avocado mixture on bread slices; add tomato slices and sprinkle with black pepper. 3. Place the Crisper Tray in the bottom position. Add the topped breads to it and close the lid. Move SmartSwitch to AIR FRY/STOVETOP, set the cooking temperature to 350°F and the cooking time to 5 minutes. 4. Transfer the breads to the plate, and top each piece with salmon, capers, and red onion. Serve warm.

Per Serving: Calories 314; Fat: 19.6g; Sodium: 709mg; Carbs: 21.48g; Fiber: 8g; Sugar: 2.97g; Protein: 16.13g

Egg "Quiche Lorraine" Cups

Prep Time: 10 minutes | Cook Time: 18 minutes | Serves: 6

3 large eggs

2 tablespoons half-and-half

⅛ teaspoon salt

⅛ teaspoon ground black pepper

2 tablespoons finely diced peeled white onion

3 slices cooked bacon, crumbled

¼ cup shredded Swiss cheese

1 medium Roma tomato, cut into 6 thin slices

1. Whisk the eggs, half-and-half, salt, and pepper in a small bowl. 2. Evenly distribute onion, bacon, and cheese among six silicone cupcake liners lightly greased with preferred cooking oil. Pour whisked eggs into cupcake liners. Top each cup with one tomato slice. 3. Place the Crisper Tray in the bottom position. Place the cups on the tray and close the lid. Move SmartSwitch to AIR FRY/STOVETOP, and then use the center front arrows to select BAKE/ROAST. Set the cooking temperature to 350°F and the cooking time to 9 minutes. 4. Transfer to a large plate and repeat with remaining egg cups. Serve warm.

Per Serving: Calories 115; Fat: 9.09g; Sodium: 157mg; Carbs: 1.52g; Fiber: 0.1g; Sugar: 0.77g; Protein: 6.45g

Cheddar Tater Tot Egg Cups

Prep Time: 15 minutes | Cook Time: 30 minutes | Serves: 4

32 gluten-free Tater Tots, frozen

4 large eggs

½ teaspoon salt

½ teaspoon ground black pepper

4 slices cooked bacon, crumbled

¼ cup finely shredded Cheddar cheese

1. Divide tots into eight silicone cupcake liners. 2. Place the Crisper Tray in the bottom position. Place the cups on the tray and close the lid. Move SmartSwitch to AIR FRY/STOVETOP, and then use the center front arrows to select BAKE/ROAST. Set the cooking temperature to 400°F and the cooking time to 9 minutes. 3. After 4 minutes of cooking time, use the back of a spoon to smoosh tots in each cup down into an even crust. 4. You may need to cook them in batches. 5. Whisk the eggs, salt, and pepper in a medium bowl. 6. Evenly distribute bacon and cheese among cooked cupcake liners. Pour egg mixture into cups and cook them for 5 minutes at the same settings. 7. Serve Warm.

Per Serving: Calories 325; Fat: 23.61g; Sodium: 786mg; Carbs: 19.81g; Fiber: 1.4g; Sugar: 0.8g; Protein: 9.48g

Cheese Spinach Frittata

Prep Time: 10 minutes | Cook Time: 15 minutes | Serves: 2

5 large eggs

¼ teaspoon salt

¼ teaspoon ground black pepper

½ cup baby spinach leaves

1 large shallot, peeled and diced

1. In a medium bowl, whisk together eggs, salt, and pepper. Stir in remaining ingredients. 2. Pour the mixture into a cake barrel lightly greased with preferred cooking oil. 3. Place the Crisper Tray in the bottom position. Place the barrel on the tray and close the lid. Move SmartSwitch to AIR FRY/STOVETOP, and then use the center front arrows to select BAKE/ROAST. Set the cooking temperature to 325°F and the cooking time to 14 minutes. 4. Once done, transfer to a cooling rack to sit for 5 minutes. 5. Slice and serve warm.

Per Serving: Calories 186; Fat: 11.93g; Sodium: 475mg; Carbs: 2.55g; Fiber: 0.4g; Sugar: 1.18g; Protein: 16.15g

Cheddar Ham Strata

Prep Time: 10 minutes | Cook Time: 15 minutes | Serves: 4

5 large eggs

¼ teaspoon salt

¼ teaspoon ground black pepper

1 teaspoon Dijon mustard

¼ cup minced peeled sweet yellow onion

¼ cup small-diced cooked ham

⅓ cup shredded Cheddar cheese

2 pieces gluten-free sandwich bread, diced

1. Beat the eggs in a medium bowl; stir in remaining ingredients. 2. Pour the mixture into a cake barrel lightly greased with preferred cooking oil. 3. Place the Crisper Tray in the bottom position. Place the barrel on the tray and close the lid. Move SmartSwitch to AIR FRY/STOVETOP, and then use the center front arrows to select BAKE/ROAST. Set the cooking temperature to 350°F and the cooking time to 14 minutes. 4. Once done, transfer to a cooling rack to sit 5 minutes. Slice and serve warm.

Per Serving: Calories 209; Fat: 11.06g; Sodium: 545mg; Carbs: 11.63g; Fiber: 1.8g; Sugar: 2.3g; Protein: 15.55g

Raisin Rice Cereal

Prep Time: 10 minutes | Cook Time: 5 minutes | Serves: 4

4 cups gluten-free rice cereal

1 cup unsweetened coconut shreds

¼ cup raisins

2 tablespoons creamy peanut butter

1 teaspoon vanilla extract

¼ cup pure maple syrup

1 tablespoon light brown sugar

2 teaspoons ground cinnamon

¼ cup almond flour

⅛ teaspoon salt

1. Combine all ingredients in a cake barrel lightly greased with preferred cooking oil. 2. Place the Crisper Tray in the bottom position. Place the barrel on the tray and close the lid. Move SmartSwitch to AIR FRY/STOVETOP, and then use the center front arrows to select BAKE/ROAST. Set the cooking temperature to 350°F and the cooking time to 5 minutes. 3. Stir the food after 3 minutes of cooking time. 4. When done, let the dish cool for 10 minutes. 5. Crumble the dish into an airtight container until ready to serve, up to five days.

Per Serving: Calories 312; Fat: 10.45g; Sodium: 446mg; Carbs: 52.94g; Fiber: 2.7g; Sugar: 25.5g; Protein: 3.66g

Hazelnut Chocolate Granola

Prep Time: 5 minutes | Cook Time: 5 minutes | Serves: 4

1 cup chopped pecans

1 cup quick-cooking oats

1 tablespoon chia seeds

1 tablespoon flaxseed

1 cup unsweetened coconut shreds

¼ cup chocolate hazelnut spread

¼ cup diced pitted dates

¼ cup honey

1 tablespoon light brown sugar

½ teaspoon vanilla extract

¼ cup hazelnut flour

2 tablespoons unsweetened powdered chocolate

⅛ teaspoon salt

1. Combine all of the ingredients in a cake barrel lightly greased with preferred cooking oil. 2. Place the Crisper Tray in the bottom position. Place the barrel on the tray and close the lid. Move SmartSwitch to AIR FRY/STOVETOP, and then use the center front arrows to select BAKE/ROAST. Set the cooking temperature to 350°F and the cooking time to 5 minutes. 3. Stir the food after 3 minutes of cooking time. 4. Once done, let the dish cool for about 10 minutes. Crumble the dish into an airtight container and wait for up to 5 days until ready to serve.

Per Serving: Calories 565; Fat: 35.2g; Sodium: 158mg; Carbs: 65.32g; Fiber: 8.1g; Sugar: 49.11g; Protein: 7.56g

Pecan Pumpkin Cereal

Prep Time: 5 minutes | Cook Time: 5 minutes | Serves: 4

1 cup unsalted pumpkin seeds

⅔ cup chopped pecans

⅓ cup quick-cooking oats

1 cup unsweetened coconut shreds

¼ cup pumpkin purée

¼ cup diced pitted dates

2 tablespoons almond butter

2 teaspoons pumpkin pie spice

¼ cup honey

1 tablespoon dark brown sugar

¼ cup coconut flour

⅛ teaspoon salt

1. Combine all the ingredients in a cake barrel lightly greased with preferred cooking oil. 2. Place the Crisper Tray in the bottom position. Place the barrel on the tray and close the lid. Move SmartSwitch to AIR FRY/STOVETOP, and then use the center front arrows to select BAKE/ROAST. Set the cooking temperature to 350°F and the cooking time to 5 minutes. 3. Stir the food after 3 minutes of cooking time. 4. Once done, let the dish cool for about 10 minutes. 5. Crumble the dish into a large airtight container until ready to serve (up to five days).

Per Serving: Calories 606; Fat: 44.49g; Sodium: 226mg; Carbs: 47.38g; Fiber: 6.4g; Sugar: 35.65g; Protein: 14.19g

Loaded Quesadillas

Prep Time: 10 minutes | Cook Time: 16 minutes | Serves: 4

8 (6") gluten-free flour tortillas

½ pound cooked bacon, crumbled

6 large eggs, scrambled

1½ cups shredded Cheddar cheese

1. Place one tortilla in bottom of a cake barrel. Evenly layer one-quarter portion each of bacon, eggs, and cheese over tortilla. Top them with second tortilla. 2. Place the Crisper Tray in the bottom position. Place the barrel on the tray and close the lid. Move SmartSwitch to AIR FRY/STOVETOP, and then use the center front arrows to select BAKE/ROAST. Set the cooking temperature to 350°F and the cooking time to 4 minutes. 3. You can cook them in batches. 4. Let the quesadillas cool for 3 minutes before slicing and serving.

Per Serving: Calories 734; Fat: 45.76g; Sodium: 1828mg; Carbs: 53.27g; Fiber: 3.8g; Sugar: 3.42g; Protein: 29.45g

Mix Trail Oatmeal

Prep Time: 10 minutes | Cook Time: 10 minutes | Serves: 4

1½ cups quick-cooking oats

⅓ cup light brown sugar

1 large egg

1 teaspoon orange zest

1 tablespoon fresh-squeezed orange juice

2 tablespoons whole milk

2 tablespoons pure maple syrup

2 tablespoons unsalted butter, melted

2 tablespoons raisins

2 tablespoons dried cranberries

⅛ teaspoon ground nutmeg

⅛ teaspoon salt

¼ cup pecan pieces

¼ cup mini chocolate chips

1. In a medium bowl, combine all ingredients except mini chocolate chips. 2. Transfer the mixture to a cake barrel lightly greased with preferred cooking oil. 3. Place the Crisper Tray in the bottom position. Place the barrel on the tray and close the lid. Move SmartSwitch to AIR FRY/STOVETOP, and then use the center front arrows to select BAKE/ROAST. Set the cooking temperature to 325°F and the cooking time to 8 minutes. 4. Once done, transfer the barrel to a cooling rack and let sit 5 minutes. Slice and serve warm garnished with chocolate chips.

Per Serving: Calories 198; Fat: 11.26g; Sodium: 93mg; Carbs: 21.41g; Fiber: 2.1g; Sugar: 8.5g; Protein: 3.99g

Buttermilk Biscuits

Prep Time: 10 minutes | Cook Time: 16 minutes | Serves: 4

2 cups gluten-free all-purpose flour

1 tablespoon baking powder

½ teaspoon baking soda

½ teaspoon xanthan gum

½ teaspoon salt

½ teaspoon granulated sugar

4 tablespoons butter, cold, cubed

1¼ cups buttermilk

1. In a small bowl, combine flour, baking powder, baking soda, xanthan gum, salt, and sugar. Add butter and buttermilk gradually until a sticky dough forms. 2. Flour your hands and then form the dough into 8 balls. 3. Arrange the balls into a greased pan. 3. Place the Crisper Tray in the bottom position. Place the pan on the tray and close the lid. Move SmartSwitch to AIR FRY/STOVETOP, and then use the center front arrows to select BAKE/ ROAST. Set the cooking temperature to 350°F and the cooking time to 8 minutes. 4. Transfer the biscuits to a large plate. Enjoy.

Per Serving: Calories 365; Fat: 12.82g; Sodium: 689mg; Carbs: 53.45g; Fiber: 1.8g; Sugar: 4.16g; Protein: 9.12g

Onion Corn Muffins

Prep Time: 10 minutes | Cook Time: 18 minutes | Serves: 8

1 cup Bob's Red Mill Gluten Free Cornbread Mix

2 teaspoons granulated sugar

⅛ teaspoon salt

¾ cup buttermilk

3 tablespoons butter, melted

1 large egg

¼ cup minced peeled yellow onion

2 beef hot dogs, sliced and cut into half-moons

1. Combine the cornbread mix, sugar, and salt in a small bowl. 2. In another small bowl, whisk together buttermilk, butter, and egg. 3. Add wet ingredients to dry ingredients and combine. Fold in minced onion and hot dog pieces. 4. Transfer the mixture to eight silicone cupcake liners lightly greased with preferred cooking oil. 5. Place the Crisper Tray in the bottom position. Place the cups on the tray and close the lid. Move SmartSwitch to AIR FRY/STOVETOP, and then use the center front arrows to select BAKE/ROAST. Set the cooking temperature to 350°F and the cooking time to 9 minutes. 6. Serve and enjoy.

Per Serving: Calories 76; Fat: 5.51g; Sodium: 156mg; Carbs: 5.17g; Fiber: 0.1g; Sugar: 1.99g; Protein: 1.76g

Caramel Banana Muffins

Prep Time: 10 minutes | Cook Time: 15 minutes | Serves: 8

1 cup gluten-free all-purpose flour

½ teaspoon baking soda

⅓ cup granulated sugar

¼ teaspoon salt

⅓ cup mashed banana, about 1 large ripe banana

½ teaspoon vanilla extract

1 large egg

1 tablespoon vegetable oil

¼ cup salted caramel chips

1. Combine the flour, baking soda, sugar, and salt in a large bowl. 2. In a separate medium bowl, combine mashed banana, vanilla, egg, and oil. 3. Pour wet ingredients into dry ingredients and gently combine. Fold in salted caramel chips. Do not overmix. 4. Spoon mixture into eight silicone cupcake liners lightly greased with preferred cooking oil. 5. Place the Crisper Tray in the bottom position. Place the cups on the tray and close the lid. Move SmartSwitch to AIR FRY/STOVETOP, and then use the center front arrows to select BAKE/ROAST. Set the cooking temperature to 375°F and the cooking time to 7 minutes. 6. Let the dish cool for a while before serving.

Per Serving: Calories 112; Fat: 2.52g; Sodium: 3697mg; Carbs: 19.76g; Fiber: 0.8g; Sugar: 6.08g; Protein: 2.56g

Toffee Zucchini Bread

Prep Time: 10 minutes | Cook Time: 20 minutes | Serves: 6

1 cup gluten-free all-purpose flour

½ teaspoon baking soda

½ cup granulated sugar

¼ teaspoon ground cinnamon

¼ teaspoon salt

⅓ cup grated zucchini

1 large egg

1 tablespoon olive oil

1 teaspoon vanilla extract

2 tablespoons English toffee bits

2 tablespoons mini chocolate chips

1. Combine all of the ingredients in a oiled spring-form pan. 2. Place the Crisper Tray in the bottom position. Place the pan on the tray and close the lid. Move SmartSwitch to AIR FRY/STOVETOP, and then use the center front arrows to select BAKE/ROAST. Set the cooking temperature to 375°F and the cooking time to 20 minutes. 3. Let the dish cool for 10 minutes. Once cooled, slice and enjoy.

Per Serving: Calories 174; Fat: 4.4g; Sodium: 240mg; Carbs: 29.85g; Fiber: 1g; Sugar: 9.86g; Protein: 3.28g

Nutty Squash Bread

Prep Time: 10 minutes | Cook Time: 20 minutes | Serves: 8

1 cup gluten-free all-purpose flour

½ teaspoon baking soda

½ cup granulated sugar

1 teaspoon ground cinnamon

1 teaspoon pumpkin pie spice

¼ teaspoon salt

½ cup canned butternut squash purée

1 large egg

1 tablespoon vegetable oil

1 tablespoon orange juice

1 teaspoon orange zest

¼ cup crushed walnuts

1. Combine all the ingredients in a greased spring-form pan. 2. Place the Crisper Tray in the bottom position. Place the molds on the tray and close the lid. Move SmartSwitch to AIR FRY/STOVETOP, and then use the center front arrows to select BAKE/ROAST. Set the cooking temperature to 375°F and the cooking time to 20 minutes. 3. Let the dish cool 10 minutes to set. Once set, remove springform sides. Slice and serve warm.

Per Serving: Calories 125; Fat: 4.12g; Sodium: 161mg; Carbs: 19.49g; Fiber: 0.9g; Sugar: 6.64g; Protein: 2.91g

Blueberry Muffins with Lemon Zest

Prep Time: 10 minutes | Cook Time: 15 minutes | Serves: 8

1 cup gluten-free all-purpose flour

½ teaspoon baking soda

⅓ cup granulated sugar

¼ teaspoon salt

1 tablespoon unsweetened applesauce

1 tablespoon lemon juice

1 teaspoon lemon zest

½ teaspoon vanilla extract

1 large egg

1 tablespoon vegetable oil

¼ cup halved fresh blueberries

1. Combine the flour, baking soda, sugar, and salt in a large bowl. 2. In a medium bowl, combine applesauce, lemon juice, lemon zest, vanilla, egg, and oil. 3. Pour wet ingredients from medium bowl into large bowl with dry ingredients. Gently combine. Fold in blueberries. Do not overmix. 4. Spoon mixture into eight silicone cupcake liners lightly greased with preferred cooking oil. 5. Place the Crisper Tray in the bottom position. Place the molds on the tray and close the lid. Move SmartSwitch to AIR FRY/STOVETOP, and then use the center front arrows to select BAKE/ROAST. Set the cooking temperature to 375°F and the cooking time to 7 minutes. 6. Let the dish cool for a while before serving.

Per Serving: Calories 106; Fat: 2.48g; Sodium: 161mg; Carbs: 18.27g; Fiber: 0.6g; Sugar: 6.01g; Protein: 2.46g

Chapter 2 Vegetable and Sides Recipes

Cauliflower with Onion

Prep Time: 5 minutes | Cook Time: 15 minutes | Serves: 3

¾ pound cauliflower florets

1 large onion, cut into wedges

2 cloves garlic, pressed

1 tablespoon olive oil

Sea salt and ground black pepper, to taste

1 teaspoon paprika

1. Toss the cauliflower florets and onion with the garlic, olive oil, and spices. Toss them until they are well coated on all sides. 2. Place the Crisper Tray in the bottom position. Add the vegetables to it and close the lid. Move SmartSwitch to AIR FRY/STOVETOP, set the cooking temperature to 400°F and the cooking time to 13 minutes. 3. Toss the food halfway through. 4. Serve hot.

Per Serving: Calories 99; Fat: 5.01g; Sodium: 38mg; Carbs: 12.8g; Fiber: 3.7g; Sugar: 5.15g; Protein: 3.26g

Hush Puppies

Prep Time: 5 minutes | Cook Time: 15 minutes | Serves: 4

1 cup (140 g) cornmeal, preferably finely ground

½ cup (63 g) all-purpose flour

1 tablespoon (13 g) granulated sugar

1 teaspoon kosher salt

½ teaspoon baking soda

½ teaspoon black pepper

1 cup (240 ml) buttermilk

2 tablespoons (28 g) unsalted butter, melted

Vegetable oil for spraying

1. Whisk the cornmeal, flour, sugar, salt, baking soda, and pepper in a medium bowl. 2. Make a well in the center of the dry ingredients. Pour in the buttermilk and melted butter and stir with a fork until the batter just comes together. 3. Let the batter rest for 10 minutes. 4. Using a small cookie scoop or spoon, scoop 5 or 6 circles of batter approximately 1½ inches. 5. Place the Crisper Tray in the bottom position. Add the food to it, spray them with oil and close the lid. Move SmartSwitch to AIR FRY/STOVETOP, set the cooking temperature to 390°F and the cooking time to 10 minutes. 6. When cooked, the outside should be firm and browned and the inside is cooked through. 7. Serve warm with butter.

Per Serving: Calories 270; Fat: 5.25g; Sodium: 861mg; Carbs: 48.28g; Fiber: 2g; Sugar: 5.57g; Protein: 6.7g

Cremini Mushroom Slices

Prep Time: 5 minutes | Cook Time: 10 minutes | Serves: 4

1 pound cremini mushrooms, sliced

2 tablespoons olive oil

½ teaspoon shallot powder

½ teaspoon garlic powder

1 tablespoon coconut aminos

1 tablespoon white wine

Sea salt and ground black pepper, to taste

1 tablespoon fresh parsley, chopped

1. Toss the mushrooms with the remaining ingredients until they are well coated on all sides. 2. Place the Crisper Tray in the bottom position. Add the mushrooms to it and close the lid. Move SmartSwitch to AIR FRY/ STOVETOP, set the cooking temperature to 400°F and the cooking time to 7 minutes. 3. Toss the food halfway through. 4. Garnish the dish with the fresh herbs, if desired.

Per Serving: Calories 87; Fat: 7.15g; Sodium: 11mg; Carbs: 4.28g; Fiber: 1.3g; Sugar: 2.42g; Protein: 3.65g

Yukon Gold Potatoes

Prep Time: 5 minutes | Cook Time: 15 minutes | Serves: 3

¾ pound Yukon Gold potatoes, peeled and cut into 1-inch chunks

1 tablespoon olive oil

Sea salt and ground black pepper, to taste

½ turmeric powder

½ teaspoon garlic powder

½ teaspoon paprika

1. Toss the potatoes with the remaining ingredients until well coated on all sides. 2. Place the Crisper Tray in the bottom position. Add the potatoes to it and close the lid. Move SmartSwitch to AIR FRY/STOVETOP, and then use the center front arrows to select BAKE/ROAST. Set the cooking temperature to 400°F and the cooking time to 13 minutes. 3. Toss the food halfway through. 4. Serve and enjoy.

Per Serving: Calories 138; Fat: 4.7g; Sodium: 9mg; Carbs: 22.17g; Fiber: 3g; Sugar: 1.72g; Protein: 2.78g

Caponata with Twist

Prep Time: 5 minutes | Cook Time: 15 minutes | Serves: 3

3 bell peppers, sliced

1 medium-sized onion, sliced

2 tablespoons olive oil

2 ounces olives, pitted and sliced

1 large tomato, sliced

1 teaspoon capers, drained

1. Toss the peppers, onion, and olive oil in a bowl. 2. Place the Crisper Tray in the bottom position. Add the food to it and close the lid. Move SmartSwitch to AIR FRY/STOVETOP, set the cooking temperature to 400°F and the cooking time to 15 minutes. 3. Toss the food after 5 minutes of cooking time; add the olives, tomato, and capers after 10 minutes of cooking time. 4. Serve and enjoy.

Per Serving: Calories 128; Fat: 12.02g; Sodium: 365mg; Carbs: 5.6g; Fiber: 1.5g; Sugar: 2.67g; Protein: 1.24g

Cheese Broccoli Florets

Prep Time: 5 minutes | Cook Time: 6 minutes | Serves: 3

¾ pound broccoli florets

1 tablespoon olive oil

½ teaspoon dried dill weed

Coarse sea salt and freshly ground black pepper, to taste

2 ounces parmesan cheese, freshly grated

1. Toss the broccoli florets with the olive oil, dill, salt, and black pepper until well coated. 2. Place the Crisper Tray in the bottom position. Add the food to it and close the lid. Move SmartSwitch to AIR FRY/STOVETOP, set the cooking temperature to 395°F and the cooking time to 6 minutes. 3. Toss the food halfway through. 4. Top the dish with the parmesan cheese and serve warm.

Per Serving: Calories 145; Fat: 10.33g; Sodium: 379mg; Carbs: 5.98g; Fiber: 3.1g; Sugar: 0.44g; Protein: 9g

Loaded Chickpea & Cauliflower Salad

Prep Time: 5 minutes | Cook Time: 15 minutes | Serves: 4

1 pound cauliflower florets

1 cup chickpeas, canned or boiled

¼ cup mayonnaise

1 teaspoon Dijon mustard

1 teaspoon ancho chili powder

Sea salt and ground black pepper, to taste

2 tablespoons fresh chives, chopped

2 tablespoons apple cider vinegar

1. Place the Crisper Tray in the bottom position. Add the cauliflower florets to it and close the lid. Move SmartSwitch to AIR FRY/STOVETOP, set the cooking temperature to 400°F and the cooking time to 12 minutes. 2. Flip the food halfway through. 3. Thoroughly combine the cauliflower florets with the remaining ingredients. 4. Serve the dish well-chilled and enjoy!

Per Serving: Calories 275; Fat: 8.28g; Sodium: 196mg; Carbs: 39.18g; Fiber: 9g; Sugar: 8.33g; Protein: 13.72g

Greek Roasted Beets

Prep Time: 5 minutes | Cook Time: 40 minutes | Serves: 4

1 pound beets, whole

Sea salt and red pepper flakes, to taste

2 tablespoons apple cider vinegar

4 tablespoons olive oil

1 teaspoon garlic powder

4 ounces feta cheese, crumbled

1. Place the Crisper Tray in the bottom position. Place the beets on it. 2. Move SmartSwitch to AIR FRY/ STOVETOP, and then use the center front arrows to select BAKE/ROAST. Set the cooking temperature to 400°F and the cooking time to 40 minutes. 3. Flip the food halfway through. 4. Let them cool completely. 5. Peel the beets and cut them into thin slices; transfer to a salad bowl. Add in the remaining ingredients and stir to combine. 6. Enjoy.

Per Serving: Calories 277; Fat: 19.67g; Sodium: 604mg; Carbs: 21.37g; Fiber: 3.2g; Sugar: 17.42g; Protein: 5.23g

Fried Okra with Lemon Wedges

Prep Time: 5 minutes | Cook Time: 10 minutes | Serves: 4 to 6

1 pound (455 g) okra pods

½ cup (63 g) all-purpose flour

1 teaspoon kosher salt

1 teaspoon black pepper

2 eggs beaten with 2 tablespoons (30 ml) water

1¼ cups (63 g) panko bread crumbs

Vegetable oil for spraying

Lemon wedges for serving

1. Trim the ends of the okra pods and cut each pod into 2 or 3 pieces depending on the length. 2. Place the flour, salt, and pepper in a large plastic bag. Add the okra pieces and shake to coat the pieces with flour. 3. Add the flour-coated pieces of okra to the egg mixture and stir with a spatula until each piece is coated. 4. Dump any remaining flour out of the plastic bag and add the panko to the bag. 5. Place the Crisper Tray in the bottom position and spray it with oil. Add the food to it and close the lid. Move SmartSwitch to AIR FRY/STOVETOP, set the cooking temperature to 375°F and the cooking time to 10 minutes. Flip the food halfway through. 6. Serve the fried okra hot with wedges of lemon and additional salt or Rémoulade sauce.

Per Serving: Calories 106; Fat: 1.92g; Sodium: 450mg; Carbs: 18.16g; Fiber: 3g; Sugar: 1.82g; Protein: 5.1g

Trimmed Yellow Beans with Tomatoes

Prep Time: 5 minutes | Cook Time: 10 minutes | Serves: 3

½ pound yellow beans, trimmed

2 small tomatoes, sliced

1 tablespoon sesame oil

Sea salt and ground black pepper, to taste

1. Toss the green beans and tomatoes with the olive oil, salt, and black pepper; toss until they are well coated. 2. Place the Crisper Tray in the bottom position. Add the vegetables to it and close the lid. Move SmartSwitch to AIR FRY/STOVETOP, set the cooking temperature to 390°F and the cooking time to 8 minutes. 3. Toss the food halfway through. 4. Adjust the seasonings, and serve immediately.

Per Serving: Calories 63; Fat: 4.66g; Sodium: 191mg; Carbs: 5.21g; Fiber: 1.3g; Sugar: 1.75g; Protein: 1.26g

Mexican Street Ears of Corn

Prep Time: 5 minutes | Cook Time: 15 minutes | Serves: 4

¼ cup (60 ml) Mexican crema

¼ cup (60 g) mayonnaise

1 lime

½ teaspoon garlic powder

Pinch cayenne pepper plus more for garnish

4 shucked ears corn

2 tablespoons (28 g) unsalted butter, melted

¼ cup (38 g) crumbled queso fresco (Mexican fresh cheese)

¼ cup (4 g) chopped cilantro

1. Whisk the crema, mayonnaise, the zest from the lime, the garlic powder, and a pinch of the cayenne pepper in a small bowl. Set aside. 2. Brush the ears of corn with the melted butter. 3. Place the Crisper Tray in the bottom position. Add the ears of corn to it and close the lid. Move SmartSwitch to AIR FRY/STOVETOP, set the cooking temperature to 400°F and the cooking time to 12 minutes. 4. Transfer the ears of corn to a serving platter. 5. Brush the ears with the crema and mayonnaise mixture. Sprinkle the crumbled queso fresco and chopped cilantro on top of the corn. 6. Spritz the corn with the juice from the lime and sprinkle with additional cayenne pepper, if desired. Serve immediately.

Per Serving: Calories 263; Fat: 14.16g; Sodium: 223mg; Carbs: 30.33g; Fiber: 4.3g; Sugar: 5.77g; Protein: 9.11g

Cherry Tomatoes with Basil

Prep Time: 10 minutes | Cook Time: 30 minutes | Serves: 4

2 pints (600 g) cherry or grape tomatoes

2 teaspoons extra-virgin olive oil

¼ teaspoon kosher salt

1 sprig basil

1. Toss the tomatoes with the olive oil and salt in a medium bowl. 2. Place the Crisper Tray in the bottom position. Add the tomatoes to it and close the lid. Move SmartSwitch to AIR FRY/STOVETOP, set the cooking temperature to 250°F and the cooking time to 30 minutes. Flip them twice during cooking. 3. The tomatoes should be softened and browned in places when cooked. 4. Transfer the tomatoes and place in a serving dish. 5. Remove the leaves from the sprig of basil and cut them into ribbons. Add the basil to the tomatoes. 6. Serve the dish warm or at room temperature.

Per Serving: Calories 11; Fat: 0.98g; Sodium: 165mg; Carbs: 0.66g; Fiber: 0.1g; Sugar: 0.53g; Protein: 0.05g

Turkish Leek Fritters

Prep Time: 5 minutes | Cook Time: 25 minutes | Serves: 4

2 tablespoons (30 ml) extra-virgin olive oil

3 leeks, white and light green parts only, sliced

Kosher salt and pepper to taste

1 egg, beaten

3 tablespoons (24 g) all-purpose flour

2 tablespoons (6 g) minced chives

¾ cup (39 g) panko bread crumbs

Vegetable oil for spraying

Lemon wedges for serving

1. Heat the olive oil in a large skillet over medium heat. Sauté the sliced leeks for 10 minutes until softened. Lower the heat as necessary, so the leeks do not brown. Season the leeks well with salt and pepper. 2. Transfer the cooked leeks to a medium bowl. Add the beaten egg, flour, and chives and stir with a fork to combine. The mixture should start to thicken and become a bit pasty. 3. Spread the panko on a plate. 4. Divide the leek mixture into 4 equal quarters and form each quarter into a patty, squeezing as necessary to get the patty to stick together. 5. Dredge the top and bottom of each patty in the panko. 6. Place the Crisper Tray in the bottom position and spray it with oil. Add the patties to it and close the lid. Move SmartSwitch to AIR FRY/STOVETOP, set the cooking temperature to 375°F and the cooking time to 13 minutes. Flip the patties and spray their tops with oil after 8 minutes of cooking. 7. Transfer the patties to a serving platter. Serve the leek patties warm with lemon wedges.

Per Serving: Calories 373; Fat: 13.96g; Sodium: 222mg; Carbs: 9.92g; Fiber: 0.6g; Sugar: 1.46g; Protein: 48.82g

Flavorful Cauliflower Florets

Prep Time: 5 minutes | Cook Time: 15 minutes | Serves: 3

¾ pound cauliflower florets

1 tablespoon olive oil

½ teaspoon dried oregano

1 teaspoon dried basil

1 teaspoon dried rosemary

Sea salt and ground black pepper, to taste

1. Toss the cauliflower florets and onion with the olive oil and spices until the vegetables are well coated on all sides. 2. Place the Crisper Tray in the bottom position. Add the food to it and close the lid. Move SmartSwitch to AIR FRY/STOVETOP, set the cooking temperature to 400°F and the cooking time to 13 minutes. 3. Toss the food halfway through. 4. Serve and enjoy.

Per Serving: Calories 70; Fat: 4.85g; Sodium: 34mg; Carbs: 5.93g; Fiber: 2.5g; Sugar: 2.18g; Protein: 2.26g

Caribbean Yuca Fries

Prep Time: 5 minutes | Cook Time: 15 minutes | Serves: 4

3 yuca roots

Vegetable oil for spraying

1 teaspoon kosher salt

1. Prepare a bowl of water. 2. Trim the ends off the yuca roots and cut each one into 2 or 3 pieces depending on the length. 3. Peel off the rough outer skin with a paring knife or sharp vegetable peeler. Halve each piece of yuca lengthwise. 4. Place the peeled pieces in a bowl of water to prevent them from oxidizing and turning brown. 5. Fill a large pot with water and bring to a boil over high heat. Add salt to the boiling water. 6. Add the yuca pieces to the water and cook them for 12 to 15 minutes until they are tender enough to be pierced with a fork, but not falling apart. 7. Drain. Some of the yuca pieces will have fibrous string running down the center. Remove it. 8. Cut the yuca into 2 or 3 pieces to resemble thick-cut french fries. 9. Place the Crisper Tray in the bottom position. Add the yuca fries to it and close the lid. Move SmartSwitch to AIR FRY/STOVETOP, set the cooking temperature to 400°F and the cooking time to 10 minutes. Flip the fries halfway through. 10. The outside of the fries should be crisp and browned and the inside fluffy. 11. Spray the cooked yuca with oil and toss with 1 teaspoon salt. 12. Serve the yuca fries warm with Toum, Chipotle Ketchup, or Mint Chimichurri.

Per Serving: Calories 64; Fat: 0.09g; Sodium: 616mg; Carbs: 14.86g; Fiber: 4.2g; Sugar: 0g; Protein: 2.24g

Italian Eggplant Slices

Prep Time: 5 minutes | Cook Time: 15 minutes | Serves: 4

2 eggs, whisked

½ cup almond flour

½ cup Parmesan cheese, grated

1 teaspoon Italian seasoning mix

¾ pound eggplant, peeled and sliced

1. Thoroughly combine the eggs, almond flour, cheese, and Italian seasoning mix in a bowl. 2. Dip the eggplant slices in the egg mixture until they are well coated on all sides. 3. Place the Crisper Tray in the bottom position. Add the eggplant slices to it and close the lid. Move SmartSwitch to AIR FRY/STOVETOP, set the cooking temperature to 400°F and the cooking time to 13 minutes. Flip the food halfway through. 4. Serve and enjoy.

Per Serving: Calories 108; Fat: 5.8g; Sodium: 311mg; Carbs: 7.35g; Fiber: 2.7g; Sugar: 3.18g; Protein: 7.21g

Coated Shishito Peppers

Prep Time: 10 minutes | Cook Time: 10 minutes | Serves: 4

1 cup (125 g) all-purpose flour

½ cup (64 g) cornstarch

2 teaspoons baking soda

1 teaspoon kosher salt

1 cup (240 ml) seltzer water or club soda

8 ounces (225 g) shishito peppers

Vegetable oil for spraying

1 To make the tempura batter, whisk together the flour, cornstarch, baking soda, and salt in a large bowl. 2. Slowly whisk in the seltzer water until you have created a thick batter. 3. Place a cooling rack over a board lined with wax or parchment paper. 4. Using the stem as handle, dip a shishito pepper in the batter then tap it against the side of the bowl several times to remove any excess. Place the battered peppers on the rack. Repeat with half the peppers, waiting to batter the other half. 5. Place the Crisper Tray in the bottom position. Add the battered peppers to it, spray them with oil and close the lid. Move SmartSwitch to AIR FRY/STOVETOP, set the cooking temperature to 350°F and the cooking time to 8 minutes. 6. The peppers should browned on the outside and tender on the inside when cooked. 7. While the peppers are cooking, batter the remaining peppers. You can cook the peppers in batches. 8. Place the peppers on a serving plate or platter. 9. Serve the peppers warm with soy-vinegar dipping sauce.

Per Serving: Calories 197; Fat: 0.43g; Sodium: 1229mg; Carbs: 43.81g; Fiber: 1.8g; Sugar: 2.98g; Protein: 4.4g

Chinese Brussels Sprouts

Prep Time: 5 minutes | Cook Time: 10 minutes | Serves: 2

½ pound Brussels sprouts, trimmed

2 tablespoons sesame oil

Sea salt and ground black pepper, to taste

1 teaspoon Five-spice powder

1 teaspoon soy sauce

1 teaspoon rice vinegar

1. Toss the Brussels sprouts with the oil until well coated on all sides. 2. Place the Crisper Tray in the bottom position. Add the food to it and close the lid. Move SmartSwitch to AIR FRY/STOVETOP, set the cooking temperature to 380°F and the cooking time to 14 minutes. 3. Toss them with the remaining ingredients after 10 minutes of cooking time. 4. Serve warm and enjoy!

Per Serving: Calories 190; Fat: 14.48g; Sodium: 71mg; Carbs: 13.91g; Fiber: 4.9g; Sugar: 4.24g; Protein: 4.6g

Maple-Soy Brussels Sprouts

Prep Time: 10 minutes | Cook Time: 30 minutes | Serves: 4

½ pounds (680 g) Brussels sprouts, trimmed and, if large, halved

1 tablespoon (15 ml) extra-virgin olive oil

½ teaspoon kosher salt

3 tablespoons (45 ml) soy sauce

2 tablespoons (40 g) maple syrup

Juice and zest of 1 lime

1 clove garlic, minced

1 tablespoon (15 ml) sriracha

1. Toss the Brussels sprouts with the olive oil and salt. 2. Place the Crisper Tray in the bottom position. Add the sprouts to it and close the lid. Move SmartSwitch to AIR FRY/STOVETOP, set the cooking temperature to 375°F and the cooking time to 20 minutes. 3. The sprouts should be browned, crispy, and fork-tender when cooked. 4. Combine the soy sauce, maple syrup, lime zest and juice, garlic, and sriracha in a small saucepan. Bring to a boil over medium heat. Reduce the heat and simmer for 5 to 7 minutes until thickened and slightly syrupy. 5. Place the Brussels sprouts in a serving bowl and drizzle the maple-soy sauce over them. Stir to coat the sprouts with the sauce and serve warm.

Per Serving: Calories 102; Fat: 3.85g; Sodium: 517mg; Carbs: 15.93g; Fiber: 2.5g; Sugar: 9.79g; Protein: 2.88g

Mediterranean Green Beans

Prep Time: 5 minutes | Cook Time: 7 minutes | Serves: 3

¾ pound green beans, cleaned and trimmed

1 tablespoon olive oil

1 clove garlic, pressed

Sea salt and ground black pepper, to taste

2 ounces feta cheese, crumbled

1 tablespoon pistachio, chopped

1. Toss the green beans with the olive oil, garlic, salt, and black pepper until they are well coated. 2. Place the Crisper Tray in the bottom position. Add the green beans to it and close the lid. Move SmartSwitch to AIR FRY/STOVETOP, set the cooking temperature to 375°F and the cooking time to 7 minutes. 3. Check the green beans halfway through. 4. When cooked, you can season them more; garnish the dish with cheese and chopped pistachio, and then enjoy.

Per Serving: Calories 137; Fat: 10.24g; Sodium: 177mg; Carbs: 8.13g; Fiber: 2.7g; Sugar: 2.63g; Protein: 4.84g

Fried Green Tomatoes

Rëmoulade

1 cup (225 g) mayonnaise

3 tablespoons (45 g) mustard

1 tablespoon (15 ml) freshly squeezed lemon juice

1 tablespoon (8.6 g) capers

1 tablespoon (1.3 g) chopped fresh flat-leaf parsley

2 scallions, white and light green part only, sliced

2 teaspoons Louisiana-style hot sauce

1½ teaspoons Cajun seasoning

½ teaspoon garlic powder

½ teaspoon black pepper

Fried Green Tomatoes

3 green tomatoes

¾ cup (94 g) all-purpose flour

¾ cup (105 g) cornmeal, preferably finely ground

1½ teaspoons kosher salt

1 teaspoon black pepper

½ teaspoon cayenne pepper

2 eggs

¼ cup (60 ml) buttermilk (regular milk is an acceptable substitute)

Vegetable oil for spraying

1. Combine all the rémoulade ingredients in a medium-size bowl. Cover the bowl and chill for at least 1 hour to allow the flavors to develop. 2. Trim the ends off each tomato and slice into ¼-inch-thick slices. Place the slices on a paper towel–lined plate to absorb excess liquid. 3. Place the flour, cornmeal, salt, black pepper, and cayenne pepper on a second plate, stirring with a fork to combine. 4. Whisk the eggs and buttermilk together in a shallow bowl. 5. Dip a third of the tomato slices in the egg mixture then dredge them in the flour-cornmeal mixture, shaking off any excess. 6. Spray both sides of the tomato slices with oil, making sure to coat the slices well. 7. Place the Crisper Tray in the bottom position. Add the tomato slices to it and close the lid. Move SmartSwitch to AIR FRY/STOVETOP, set the cooking temperature to 400°F and the cooking time to 10 minutes. 8. Flip the slices halfway through. 9. You can cook them in batches for better taste. 10. Serve the fried green tomatoes hot out of the fryer with rémoulade sauce.

Per Serving: Calories 678; Fat: 31.12g; Sodium: 1765mg; Carbs: 52.23g; Fiber: 4.6g; Sugar: 6.37g; Protein: 45.22g

Steak Fries

Prep Time: 10 minutes | Cook Time: 25 minutes | Serves: 4

2 pounds (910 g) russet potatoes, cut into ½-inch-thick (1.3 cm) fries

1 cup (136 g) garlic cloves, peeled

3 teaspoons kosher salt, divided

5 to 6 tablespoons (75 to 90 ml) freshly squeezed lemon juice, chilled or iced, divided

2½ cups (600 ml) canola or other neutral oil, chilled, divided, plus 1 tablespoon (15 ml)

1. Place the potato slices in a large bowl and cover with cold water. Soak them for at least 30 minutes and up to several hours to remove excess starch. 2. Place the garlic cloves in a food processor along with 2 teaspoons of the salt. Pulse several times, scraping down the sides of the bowl as necessary, until the garlic is finely minced. Add 1 tablespoon of lemon juice and pulse again until a paste forms. 3. With the motor running, slowly add ½ cup of the oil in a steady stream. Add an additional tablespoon of lemon juice and pulse. Then, with the motor running, slowly add a second ½ cup of oil followed by the third tablespoon of lemon juice. 4. Repeat this process until you have used all the oil. Transfer the toum to a serving bowl or container, if not using right away, and refrigerate until needed. 5. Drain the potatoes and pat dry. Toss with the remaining 1 tablespoon of oil and remaining teaspoon of salt. 6. Place the Crisper Tray in the bottom position. Add the potatoes to it and close the lid. Move SmartSwitch to AIR FRY/STOVETOP, set the cooking temperature to 375°F and the cooking time to 25 minutes. 7. Toss them every 5 minutes during cooking. 8. You can cook them in batches. 9. The potatoes should be browned on all sides and crispy when done. 9. Toss the potatoes with additional salt, if desired. Serve the steak fries immediately with toum for dipping.

Per Serving: Calories 391; Fat: 18.12g; Sodium: 1761mg; Carbs: 53.54g; Fiber: 3.7g; Sugar: 2.23g; Protein: 7.08g

Seasoned Turkey Breast

Prep Time: 5 minutes | Cook Time: 60 minutes | Serves: 6-8

Pepper and salt

1 oven-ready turkey breast

Turkey seasonings of choice

1. Season the turkey breast with pepper, salt, and other desired seasonings. 2. Place the Crisper Tray in the bottom position. Add the turkey breast to it and close the lid. Move SmartSwitch to AIR FRY/STOVETOP, set the cooking temperature to 350°F and the cooking time to 60 minutes. 3. The meat should have an internal temperature of 165°F when cooked. 4. Let the dish cool for 10 to 15 minutes before slicing and serving.

Per Serving: Calories 324; Fat: 4.4g; Sodium: 1797mg; Carbs: 10.84g; Fiber: 2.4g; Sugar: 2.38g; Protein: 57.67g

Keto "Mock KFC" Chicken

Prep Time: 25 minutes | Cook Time: 20 minutes | Serves: 6

1 teaspoon chili flakes

1 teaspoon curcumin

1 teaspoon white pepper

1 teaspoon ginger powder

1 teaspoon garlic powder

1 teaspoon paprika

1 teaspoon powdered mustard

1 teaspoon pepper

1 tablespoon celery salt

⅓ teaspoon oregano

½ tablespoon basil

½ teaspoon thyme

2 garlic cloves

1 egg

6 boneless, skinless chicken thighs

2 tablespoon unsweetened almond milk

¼ C. whey protein isolate powder

1. Wash and pat dry chicken thighs, and then slice them into small chunks. 2. Mash cloves and add them along with all spices in a blender. Blend them until smooth and pour over chicken, adding milk and egg. 3. Cover chicken and chill for 1 hour. 4. Add whey protein to a bowl and dredge coated chicken pieces. Shake excess powder. 5. Place the Crisper Tray in the bottom position. Add the meat to it and close the lid. Move SmartSwitch to AIR FRY/STOVETOP, set the cooking temperature to 390°F and the cooking time to 20 minutes. 6. Flip the food halfway through. 7. Serve and enjoy.

Per Serving: Calories 269; Fat: 13.8g; Sodium: 471mg; Carbs: 10.48g; Fiber: 1g; Sugar: 1.04g; Protein: 25.06g

Cheese Chicken Fritters

Prep Time: 25 minutes | Cook Time: 20 minutes | Serves: 6

Chicken Fritters:

½ teaspoon salt

⅛ teaspoon pepper

1½ tablespoons fresh dill

1⅓ C. shredded mozzarella cheese

⅓ C. coconut flour

⅓ C. vegan mayo

2 eggs

1 ½ pounds chicken breasts

Garlic Dip:

⅛ teaspoon pepper

¼ teaspoon salt

½ tablespoon lemon juice

1 pressed garlic cloves

⅓ C. vegan mayo

1. Slice chicken breasts into ⅓-inch pieces and place in a bowl. 2. Add all remaining fritter ingredients to the bowl and stir well. Cover the bowl and chill the chicken pieces for 2 hours or overnight. 3. Place the Crisper Tray in the bottom position. Add the food to it and close the lid. Move SmartSwitch to AIR FRY/STOVETOP, set the cooking temperature to 350°F and the cooking time to 20 minutes. Flip the pieces halfway through. 4. To make the dipping sauce, combine all the dip ingredients until smooth. 5. Serve the meat with the sauce

Per Serving: Calories 310; Fat: 17.83g; Sodium: 482mg; Carbs: 6.46g; Fiber: 0.8g; Sugar: 4.2g; Protein: 29.87g

Classic Thanksgiving Turkey Breasts

Prep Time: 15 minutes | Cook Time: 60 minutes | Serves: 4

1 tablespoon butter, room temperature

Kosher salt and ground black pepper, to taste

1 teaspoon cayenne pepper

1 teaspoon Italian herb mix

1 pound turkey breast, bone-in

1. Thoroughly combine the butter, salt, black pepper, cayenne pepper, and herb mix in a bowl. 2. Rub the mixture all over the turkey breast. 3. Place the Crisper Tray in the bottom position. Add the turkey breast to it and close the lid. Move SmartSwitch to AIR FRY/STOVETOP, set the cooking temperature to 350°F and the cooking time to 60 minutes. 4. Flip the breast every 20 minutes. 5. Serve and enjoy.

Per Serving: Calories 209; Fat: 10.94g; Sodium: 91mg; Carbs: 1.32g; Fiber: 0.3g; Sugar: 0.62g; Protein: 25.13g

Keto Chicken Breasts

Prep Time: 15 minutes | Cook Time: 10 minutes | Serves: 4

½ C. keto marinara

6 tablespoon mozzarella cheese

1 tablespoon melted ghee

2 tablespoon grated parmesan cheese

6 tablespoon gluten-free seasoned breadcrumbs

2 8-ounce chicken breasts

1. Mix parmesan cheese and breadcrumbs in a bowl. 2. Brush melted ghee onto the chicken and dip into breadcrumb mixture. 3. Place the Crisper Tray in the bottom position. Add the chicken to it and close the lid. Move SmartSwitch to AIR FRY/STOVETOP, set the cooking temperature to 360°F and the cooking time to 9 minutes. 4. Top each breast with a tablespoon of sauce and 1½ tablespoons of mozzarella cheese after 6 minutes of cooking time. 5. Keep cooked pieces warm as you repeat the process with remaining breasts.

Per Serving: Calories 355; Fat: 19.4g; Sodium: 1445mg; Carbs: 12.37g; Fiber: 2.3g; Sugar: 4.83g; Protein: 29.17g

Jerk Chicken Wings

Prep Time: 10 minutes | Cook Time: 16 minutes | Serves: 6-8

1 teaspoon salt

½ C. red wine vinegar

5 tablespoon lime juice

4 chopped scallions

1 tablespoon grated ginger

2 tablespoon brown sugar

1 tablespoon chopped thyme

1 teaspoon white pepper

1 teaspoon cayenne pepper

1 teaspoon cinnamon

1 tablespoon allspice

1 Habanero pepper (seeds/ribs removed and chopped finely)

6 chopped garlic cloves

2 tablespoon low-sodium soy sauce

2 tablespoon olive oil

4 pounds of chicken wings

1. Combine all ingredients except wings in a bowl. Pour them into a gallon bag and add chicken wings. 2. Chill the chicken wings with the marinade for 2 to 24 hours. 3. Place chicken wings into a strainer to drain excess liquids. 4. Place the Crisper Tray in the bottom position. Add the chicken wings to it and close the lid. Move SmartSwitch to AIR FRY/STOVETOP, set the cooking temperature to 390°F and the cooking time to 16 minutes. Flip the chicken wings halfway through. 5. Serve hot.

Per Serving: Calories 344; Fat: 11.58g; Sodium: 606mg; Carbs: 6.2g; Fiber: 0.9g; Sugar: 2.66g; Protein: 50.73g

Chicken Fingers

1½ pounds chicken tenders

1 tablespoon olive oil

1 egg, whisked

1 teaspoon fresh parsley, minced

1 teaspoon garlic, minced

Sea salt and black pepper, to taste

1 cup breadcrumbs

1. Pat the chicken dry with kitchen towels. 2. Thoroughly combine the oil, egg, parsley, garlic, salt, and black pepper in a bowl. 3. Dip the chicken tenders into the egg mixture. Then, roll the chicken over the breadcrumbs. 4. Place the Crisper Tray in the bottom position. Add the chicken tenders to it and close the lid. Move SmartSwitch to AIR FRY/STOVETOP, set the cooking temperature to 360°F and the cooking time to 10 minutes. Flip the food halfway through. 5. Serve hot.

Per Serving: Calories 503; Fat: 26.67g; Sodium: 818mg; Carbs: 35.59g; Fiber: 0.4g; Sugar: 1.12g; Protein: 30.25g

Butter Chicken Breasts

1 pound chicken breasts raw, boneless and skinless

1 tablespoon butter, room temperature

1 teaspoon garlic powder

Kosher salt and ground black pepper, to taste

1 teaspoon dried parsley flakes

1 teaspoon smoked paprika

½ teaspoon dried oregano

1. Pat the chicken dry with kitchen towels. Toss the chicken breasts with the remaining ingredients. 2. Place the Crisper Tray in the bottom position. Add the chicken breasts to it and close the lid. Move SmartSwitch to AIR FRY/STOVETOP, set the cooking temperature to 380°F and the cooking time to 12 minutes. Flip the food halfway through. 3. Serve and enjoy. Cook the chicken at 380 degrees F for 12 minutes, turning them over halfway through the cooking time. Bon appétit!

Per Serving: Calories 225; Fat: 13.46g; Sodium: 95mg; Carbs: 1g; Fiber: 0.3g; Sugar: 0.09g; Protein: 23.91g

Simple Chicken Thighs

Prep Time: 5 minutes | Cook Time: 25 minutes | Serves: 4

1 pound chicken thighs, bone-in

Sea salt and freshly ground black pepper, to taste

2 tablespoons olive oil

1 teaspoon stone-ground mustard

¼ cup hot sauce

1. Pat the chicken dry with kitchen towels. 2. Toss the chicken with the remaining ingredients. 3. Place the Crisper Tray in the bottom position. Add the chicken thighs to it and close the lid. Move SmartSwitch to AIR FRY/ STOVETOP, set the cooking temperature to 380°F and the cooking time to 22 minutes. Flip the chicken thighs halfway through. 4. Serve and enjoy.

Per Serving: Calories 314; Fat: 25.82g; Sodium: 473mg; Carbs: 0.68g; Fiber: 0.1g; Sugar: 0.22g; Protein: 18.94g

Typical Chicken Legs

Prep Time: 5 minutes | Cook Time: 30 minutes | Serves: 4

4 chicken legs, bone-in

2 tablespoons sesame oil

Coarse sea salt and ground black pepper, to taste

½ teaspoon mustard seeds

1 teaspoon cayenne pepper

½ teaspoon onion powder

½ teaspoon garlic powder

1. Pat the chicken dry with paper towels. 2. Toss the chicken legs with the remaining ingredients. 3. Place the Crisper Tray in the bottom position. Add the chicken legs to it and close the lid. Move SmartSwitch to AIR FRY/ STOVETOP, set the cooking temperature to 380°F and the cooking time to 30 minutes. 4. Flip the chicken legs halfway through. 5. Serve and enjoy.

Per Serving: Calories 1388; Fat: 18.18g; Sodium: 256mg; Carbs: 1.92g; Fiber: 0.4g; Sugar: 0.67g; Protein: 51.22g

Asian-Style Duck Breast

Prep Time: 5 minutes | Cook Time: 30 minutes | Serves: 3

1 pound duck breast

1 tablespoon Hoisin sauce

1 tablespoon Five-spice powder

Sea salt and black pepper, to taste

¼ teaspoon ground cinnamon

1. Pat the duck breasts dry with paper towels. 2. Toss the duck breast with the remaining ingredients. 3. Place the Crisper Tray in the bottom position. Add the duck breast to it and close the lid. Move SmartSwitch to AIR FRY/STOVETOP, set the cooking temperature to 330°F and the cooking time to 30 minutes. 4. Flip the duck breast halfway through. 5. Let the dish rest for 10 minutes before carving and serving.

Per Serving: Calories 206; Fat: 6.63g; Sodium: 174mg; Carbs: 4.38g; Fiber: 0.6g; Sugar: 1.61g; Protein: 30.44g

Palatable Chicken Burgers

Prep Time: 5 minutes | Cook Time: 20 minutes | Serves: 3

¾ pound chicken, ground

¼ cup tortilla chips, crushed

¼ cup Parmesan cheese, grated

1 egg, beaten

2 tablespoons onion, minced

2 garlic cloves, minced

1 tablespoon BBQ sauce

1. Mix all the ingredients until everything is well combined. 2. Form the mixture into three patties. 3. Place the Crisper Tray in the bottom position. Add the patties to it and close the lid. Move SmartSwitch to AIR FRY/STOVETOP, set the cooking temperature to 380°F and the cooking time to 17 minutes. 4. Flip the patties halfway through. 5. Serve and enjoy.

Per Serving: Calories 211; Fat: 8.62g; Sodium: 312mg; Carbs: 3.18g; Fiber: 0.3g; Sugar: 0.76g; Protein: 28.7g

Carrot Chicken Salad

Prep Time: 5 minutes | Cook Time: 15 minutes | Serves: 3

1 pound chicken breast

2 tablespoons scallions, chopped

1 carrot, shredded

½ cup mayonnaise

1 tablespoon mustard

Sea salt and ground black pepper, to taste

1. Pat the chicken dry with kitchen towels. 2. Place the Crisper Tray in the bottom position and spray it with oil. Add the chicken breast to it and close the lid. Move SmartSwitch to AIR FRY/STOVETOP, set the cooking temperature to 380°F and the cooking time to 12 minutes. 3. Flip the breast halfway through. 4. Chop the chicken breasts and transfer it to a salad bowl; add in the remaining ingredients and toss to combine well. 5. Enjoy.

Per Serving: Calories 402; Fat: 26.93g; Sodium: 477mg; Carbs: 3.79g; Fiber: 1.3g; Sugar: 1.45g; Protein: 34.37g

Paprika Chicken Cutlets

Prep Time: 5 minutes | Cook Time: 15 minutes | Serves: 4

1 pound chicken breasts, boneless, skinless, cut into 4 pieces

1 tablespoon butter, melted

1 teaspoon smoked paprika

Kosher salt and ground black pepper, to taste

1 teaspoon garlic powder

1. Flatten the chicken breasts to ¼-inch thickness. 2. Toss the chicken breasts with the remaining ingredients. 3. Place the Crisper Tray in the bottom position. Add the chicken breaat to it and close the lid. Move SmartSwitch to AIR FRY/STOVETOP, set the cooking temperature to 380°F and the cooking time to 12 minutes. 4. Flip the breast halfway through. 5. Serve and enjoy.

Per Serving: Calories 229; Fat: 13.47g; Sodium: 96mg; Carbs: 1.94g; Fiber: 0.4g; Sugar: 0.65g; Protein: 24.11g

Roll Chicken Sliders

Prep Time: 5 minutes | Cook Time: 20 minutes | Serves: 3

¾ pound chicken, ground

1 teaspoon garlic, minced

1 small onion, minced

2 tablespoons fresh parsley, minced

2 tablespoons fresh cilantro, minced

½ teaspoon mustard seeds

½ teaspoon ground cumin

½ teaspoon paprika

Sea salt and ground black pepper, to taste

2 tablespoons olive oil

6 Hawaiian rolls

1. Mix all the ingredients except for the burger buns in a bowl until everything is well combined. 2. Shape the mixture into six patties. 3. Place the Crisper Tray in the bottom position. Add the patties to it and close the lid. Move SmartSwitch to AIR FRY/STOVETOP, set the cooking temperature to 380°F and the cooking time to 17 minutes. 4. Flip the patties halfway through. 5. Serve the burgers over Hawaiian rolls and garnish with toppings of choice. Bon appétit!

Per Serving: Calories 461; Fat: 15.56g; Sodium: 510mg; Carbs: 46.59g; Fiber: 2.7g; Sugar: 7.21g; Protein: 32.26g

Mediterranean Chicken Fillets

Prep Time: 5 minutes | Cook Time: 15 minutes | Serves: 4

1½ pounds chicken fillets

1 tablespoon olive oil

1 teaspoon garlic, minced

1 tablespoon Greek seasoning mix

½ teaspoon red pepper flakes, crushed

Sea salt and ground black pepper, to taste

1. Pat the chicken dry with paper towels. 2. Toss the chicken with the remaining ingredients. 3. Place the Crisper Tray in the bottom position. Add the chicken to it and close the lid. Move SmartSwitch to AIR FRY/STOVETOP, set the cooking temperature to 380°F and the cooking time to 12 minutes. 4. Flip the chicken halfway through. 5. Serve and enjoy.

Per Serving: Calories 532; Fat: 22.61g; Sodium: 1227mg; Carbs: 57.05g; Fiber: 3.3g; Sugar: 5.77g; Protein: 23.97g

Mexican-Style Chicken Taquitos

Prep Time: 5 minutes | Cook Time: 18 minutes | Serves: 5

¾ pound chicken breasts, boneless and skinless

Kosher salt and ground black pepper, to taste

½ teaspoon red chili powder

5 small corn tortillas

5 ounces Cotija cheese, crumbled

1. Pat the chicken dry with kitchen towels. 2. Toss the chicken breasts with the salt, pepper, and red chili powder. 3. Place the Crisper Tray in the bottom position. Add the chicken breasts to it and close the lid. Move SmartSwitch to AIR FRY/STOVETOP, set the cooking temperature to 380°F and the cooking time to 12 minutes. 4. Flip the chicken breasts halfway through. 5. Place the shredded chicken and cheese on one end of each tortilla. 6. Roll them up tightly and transfer them to the cooking pot. 7. Bake the taquitos at 360°F for 6 minutes. 8. Serve and enjoy.

Per Serving: Calories 256; Fat: 13.06g; Sodium: 523mg; Carbs: 14.18g; Fiber: 1.7g; Sugar: 2.77g; Protein: 20.43g

Hawaiian Chicken Legs with Pineapple

Prep Time: 5 minutes | Cook Time: 35 minutes | Serves: 4

1 pound chicken legs, boneless

Kosher salt and freshly ground black pepper, to taste

2 tablespoons tamari sauce

1 tablespoon hot sauce

1 cup pineapple, peeled and diced

1 tablespoon fresh cilantro, roughly chopped

1. Pat the chicken dry with paper towels. 2. Toss the chicken legs with the salt, black pepper, tamari sauce, and hot sauce. 3. Place the Crisper Tray in the bottom position. Add the chicken legs to it and close the lid. Move SmartSwitch to AIR FRY/STOVETOP, set the cooking temperature to 380°F and the cooking time to 35 minutes. 4. Flip the chicken legs after 15 minutes of cooking time. 5. Top the chicken with pineapple after 30 minutes of cooking time. 6. Garnish the dish with fresh cilantro and enjoy.

Per Serving: Calories 177; Fat: 4.86g; Sodium: 205mg; Carbs: 10.69g; Fiber: 0.7g; Sugar: 9.53g; Protein: 22.2g

Delectable Chicken Fajitas

Prep Time: 10 minutes | Cook Time: 30 minutes | Serves: 4

1 pound chicken legs, boneless, skinless, cut into pieces

2 tablespoons canola oil

1 red bell pepper, sliced

1 yellow bell pepper, sliced

1 jalapeno pepper, sliced

1 onion, sliced

½ teaspoon onion powder

½ teaspoon garlic powder

Sea salt and ground black pepper, to taste

1. Pat the chicken dry with paper towels. 2. Toss the chicken legs with 1 tablespoon of the canola oil. 3. Place the Crisper Tray in the bottom position. Add the chicken legs to it and close the lid. Move SmartSwitch to AIR FRY/STOVETOP, set the cooking temperature to 380°F and the cooking time to 15 minutes. 4. Flip the chicken legs halfway through. 5. When the cooking time is up, add the remaining ingredients and adjust the cooking temperature to 400°F, then cook them for 15 minutes more. 6. Serve and enjoy.

Per Serving: Calories 219; Fat: 11.95g; Sodium: 111mg; Carbs: 4.91g; Fiber: 0.8g; Sugar: 0.87g; Protein: 22.56g

Dijon Turkey Wings

Prep Time: 15 minutes | Cook Time: 40 minutes | Serves: 5

2 pounds turkey wings, bone-in

2 garlic cloves, minced

1 small onion, chopped

1 tablespoon Dijon mustard

½ cup red wine

Sea salt and ground black pepper, to taste

1 teaspoon poultry seasoning

1. Place the turkey wings, garlic, onion, mustard, and wine in a ceramic bowl. 2. Cover the bowl and let the turkey marinate in your refrigerator overnight. 3. Discard the marinade and toss the turkey wings with the salt, black pepper, and poultry seasoning. 4. Place the Crisper Tray in the bottom position. Add the turkey wings to it and close the lid. Move SmartSwitch to AIR FRY/STOVETOP, set the cooking temperature to 400°F and the cooking time to 40 minutes. 5. Flip the turkey wings halfway through. 6. Serve and enjoy.

Per Serving: Calories 376; Fat: 22.52g; Sodium: 138mg; Carbs: 3g; Fiber: 0.6g; Sugar: 1.1g; Protein: 37.25g

Lime Duck Breast

Prep Time: 10 minutes | Cook Time: 30 minutes | Serves: 4

2 tablespoons fresh lime juice

1½ pounds duck breast

2 tablespoons olive oil

1 teaspoon cayenne pepper

Kosher salt and freshly ground black pepper, to taste

1. Pat the duck breasts dry with paper towels. 2. Toss the duck breast with the remaining ingredients. 3. Place the Crisper Tray in the bottom position. Add the duck breast to it and close the lid. Move SmartSwitch to AIR FRY/ STOVETOP, set the cooking temperature to 330°F and the cooking time to 15 minutes. 4. Flip the duck breast halfway through. 5. Adjust the cooking temperature to 350°F and cook them for 15 minutes more. 6. Let the duck breasts rest for 10 minutes before carving and serving.

Per Serving: Calories 272; Fat: 14.06g; Sodium: 97mg; Carbs: 0.91g; Fiber: 0.2g; Sugar: 0.17g; Protein: 33.85g

Fried Chicken Fillets

Prep Time: 5 minutes | Cook Time: 15 minutes | Serves: 4

1 pound chicken fillets

1 egg

1 tablespoon olive oil

1 cup crackers, crushed

1 tablespoon fresh coriander, minced

1 tablespoon fresh parsley, minced

Sea salt and ground black pepper, to taste

¼ teaspoon ground cumin

¼ teaspoon mustard seeds

1 teaspoon celery seeds

1. Pat the chicken fillets dry with paper towels. Whisk the egg in a shallow bowl. 2. Mix the remaining ingredients in a separate shallow bowl. 3. Dip the chicken breasts into the egg mixture. Then, roll the chicken breasts over the breadcrumb mixture. 4. Place the Crisper Tray in the bottom position. Add the chicken fillets to it and close the lid. Move SmartSwitch to AIR FRY/STOVETOP, set the cooking temperature to 380°F and the cooking time to 12 minutes. 5. Flip the chicken fillets halfway through. 6. Serve and enjoy.

Per Serving: Calories 196; Fat: 9.27g; Sodium: 118mg; Carbs: 1.13g; Fiber: 0.2g; Sugar: 0.25g; Protein: 25.53g

Chinese Stir-Fry Chicken

¾ C. potato starch

¼ teaspoon pepper

½ teaspoon salt

Stir-fry:

¼ teaspoon pepper

1 teaspoon sea salt

2 tablespoon avocado oil

1 egg white

14-20 chicken wing pieces

2 trimmed scallions

2 jalapeno peppers

1. Whisk pepper, salt, and egg white in a bowl until foamy. 2. Pat wings dry and add to the bowl of egg white mixture. Coat well. Let the chicken wings marinate at least 20 minutes. 3. Place coated wings in a big bowl and add starch. Dredge wings well and then shake off. 4. Place the Crisper Tray in the bottom position and spray it with oil. Add the chicken wings to it and close the lid. Move SmartSwitch to AIR FRY/STOVETOP, set the cooking temperature to 380°F and the cooking time to 30 minutes. 5. Adjust the cooking temperature to 400°F after 25 minutes of cooking time. 6. For stir fry, remove seeds from jalapenos and chop up scallions. Add both to bowl and set to the side. 7. Heat a wok with oil and add pepper, salt, scallions, and jalapenos, and cook them for 1 minute. 8. Add air fried chicken to skillet and toss with stir-fried veggies; cook them for 1 minute. 9. Serve hot.

Per Serving: Calories 125; Fat: 5.73g; Sodium: 495mg; Carbs: 3.26g; Fiber: 0.5g; Sugar: 0.51g; Protein: 14.43g

Chapter 4 Beef, Pork, and Lamb Recipes

Coconut Steak

2-pounds beef steak

3 tablespoons coconut oil

1 teaspoon coconut shred

1 teaspoon dried basil

1. Rub the beef steak with coconut shred and dried basil, and then brush the steak with coconut oil. 2. Place the Crisper Tray in the bottom position. Add the food to it and close the lid. Move SmartSwitch to AIR FRY/STOVETOP, set the cooking temperature to 390°F and the cooking time to 16 minutes. 3. Flip the steak halfway through. 4. Serve and enjoy.

Per Serving: Calories 406; Fat: 22.71g; Sodium: 133mg; Carbs: 0.13g; Fiber: 0.1g; Sugar: 0.04g; Protein: 47.97g

Parsley Beef Bread

2-pounds ground beef

1 teaspoon minced garlic

1 tablespoon dried parsley

1 teaspoon ground turmeric

¼ cup coconut flour

1 tablespoon coconut oil, softened

1. Mix ground beef with minced garlic, dried parsley, ground turmeric, and coconut flour in a bowl. 2. Place the Crisper Tray in the bottom position and spray it with oil. 3. Add the food to it, flatten the gently, and close the lid. Move SmartSwitch to AIR FRY/STOVETOP, set the cooking temperature to 370°F and the cooking time to 25 minutes. 4. Serve and enjoy.

Per Serving: Calories 521; Fat: 28.64g; Sodium: 155mg; Carbs: 1.35g; Fiber: 0.4g; Sugar: 0.43g; Protein: 60.63g

Cream Beef Bites

Prep Time: 10 minutes | Cook Time: 30 minutes | Serves: 4

2-pound beef fillet

1 tablespoon onion powder

¼ cup heavy cream

½ teaspoon salt

1 teaspoon olive oil

1. Cut the beef fillet into bites and sprinkle with onion powder and salt. 2. Place the Crisper Tray in the bottom position. Add the beef bites to it and close the lid. Move SmartSwitch to AIR FRY/STOVETOP, set the cooking temperature to 360°F and the cooking time to 30 minutes. 3. Flip the beef bites halfway through. 4. Serve and enjoy.

Per Serving: Calories 343; Fat: 16.87g; Sodium: 490mg; Carbs: 1.57g; Fiber: 0.3g; Sugar: 0.32g; Protein: 46.87g

Beef Steak Strips

Prep Time: 10 minutes | Cook Time: 35 minutes | Serves: 4

2-pounds beef steak, cut into strips

¼ cup plain yogurt

1 teaspoon lemon juice

1 teaspoon white pepper

½ teaspoon dried oregano

Cooking spray

1. Mix plain yogurt with lemon juice, white pepper, and dried oregano. 2. Then put beef strips in the plain yogurt mixture. 3. Place the Crisper Tray in the bottom position. Add the food to it and close the lid. Move SmartSwitch to AIR FRY/STOVETOP, set the cooking temperature to 360°F and the cooking time to 35 minutes. 4. Toss the food halfway through. 5. Serve and enjoy.

Per Serving: Calories 329; Fat: 13.02g; Sodium: 139mg; Carbs: 1.3g; Fiber: 0.2g; Sugar: 0.75g; Protein: 48.53g

BBQ Beef Steaks

4 beef steaks

1 cup keto BBQ sauce

1 tablespoon olive oil

1. Mix olive oil with BBQ sauce. 2. Then mix beef steaks with sauce mixture. 3. Place the Crisper Tray in the bottom position. Add the food to it and close the lid. Move SmartSwitch to AIR FRY/STOVETOP, set the cooking temperature to 400°F and the cooking time to 15 minutes. 4. Serve and enjoy.

Per Serving: Calories 375; Fat: 16.32g; Sodium: 593mg; Carbs: 4.37g; Fiber: 1.2g; Sugar: 2.56g; Protein: 50.23g

Minced Beef & Pepper Bowl

1 cup bell pepper, diced

1-pound ground beef

1 garlic clove, diced

1 teaspoon dried oregano

1 teaspoon coconut oil

1 tablespoon cream cheese

1. Mix all ingredients from the list above in the mixing bowl. 2. Place the Crisper Tray in the bottom position. Add the food to it and close the lid. Move SmartSwitch to AIR FRY/STOVETOP, set the cooking temperature to 360°F and the cooking time to 30 minutes. 3. Serve and enjoy.

Per Serving: Calories 270; Fat: 14.82g; Sodium: 87mg; Carbs: 1.62g; Fiber: 0.3g; Sugar: 0.72g; Protein: 30.75g

Mushroom Beef Roll

Prep Time: 20 minutes | Cook Time: 40 minutes | Serves: 4

1-pound beef loin

2 oz. mushrooms, chopped

1 teaspoon onion powder

1 oz. bacon, chopped, cooked

½ teaspoon dried dill

1 teaspoon chili powder

1 tablespoon avocado oil

½ teaspoon cream cheese

1. Beat the beef loin with the help of the kitchen hammer to get the flat loin. 2. Mix mushrooms with onion powder, bacon, dried dill, chili powder, and cream cheese. 3. Put the mixture over the beef loin and roll it. 4. Secure the beef roll with toothpicks and brush with avocado oil. 5. Place the Crisper Tray in the bottom position. Add the beef roll to it and close the lid. Move SmartSwitch to AIR FRY/STOVETOP, set the cooking temperature to 370°F and the cooking time to 40 minutes. 6. Serve and enjoy.

Per Serving: Calories 317; Fat: 23.02g; Sodium: 186mg; Carbs: 1.89g; Fiber: 0.7g; Sugar: 0.39g; Protein: 24.79g

Garlicky Beef Steak

Prep Time: 10 minutes | Cook Time: 15 minutes | Serves: 4

4 beef steaks

1 teaspoon garlic powder

1 tablespoon coconut oil

1. Mix beef steaks with garlic powder and coconut oil. 2. Place the Crisper Tray in the bottom position. Add the food to it and close the lid. Move SmartSwitch to AIR FRY/STOVETOP, set the cooking temperature to 400°F and the cooking time to 14 minutes. 3. Flip the steaks halfway through. 4. Serve and enjoy.

Per Serving: Calories 358; Fat: 16.24g; Sodium: 136mg; Carbs: 0.56g; Fiber: 0.1g; Sugar: 0.02g; Protein: 49.36g

Za'atar Beef

Prep Time: 10 minutes | Cook Time: 11 minutes | Serves: 6

6 beef chops

1 tablespoon coconut oil, melted

1 tablespoon za'atar seasonings

1. Mix za'atar seasonings with coconut oil. 2. Brush the beef chops with coconut oil mixture. 3. Place the Crisper Tray in the bottom position. Add the food to it and close the lid. Move SmartSwitch to AIR FRY/STOVETOP, set the cooking temperature to 400°F and the cooking time to 11 minutes. 4. Serve and enjoy.

Per Serving: Calories 168; Fat: 3.63g; Sodium: 93mg; Carbs: 31.51g; Fiber: 2.3g; Sugar: 17.77g; Protein: 3.62g

Rib Eye Steaks

Prep Time: 10 minutes | Cook Time: 25 minutes | Serves: 4

3-pound rib-eye steak

1 tablespoon keto tomato paste

1 tablespoon avocado oil

1 teaspoon salt

1 teaspoon cayenne pepper

1. Mix tomato paste with avocado oil, salt, and cayenne pepper in a bowl. 2. Coat the beef with tomato mixture. 3. Place the Crisper Tray in the bottom position. Add the food to it and close the lid. Move SmartSwitch to AIR FRY/STOVETOP, set the cooking temperature to 380°F and the cooking time to 24 minutes. 4. Flip the meat halfway through. 5. Serve and enjoy.

Per Serving: Calories 920; Fat: 74.9g; Sodium: 778mg; Carbs: 1.01g; Fiber: 0.3g; Sugar: 0.53g; Protein: 61.19g

Dijon Beef Loin

4-pounds beef loin

2 tablespoon Dijon mustard

1 tablespoon olive oil

½ tablespoon apple cider vinegar

1. Mix mustard with olive oil and apple cider vinegar. 2. Rub the beef loin with mustard mixture. 3. Place the Crisper Tray in the bottom position. Add the food to it and close the lid. Move SmartSwitch to AIR FRY/ STOVETOP, set the cooking temperature to 375°F and the cooking time to 40 minutes. 4. Flip the beef loin halfway through. 5. Serve and enjoy.

Per Serving: Calories 601; Fat: 41.06g; Sodium: 184mg; Carbs: 0.38g; Fiber: 0.2g; Sugar: 0.15g; Protein: 53.54g

Curry Beef Chops

2-pounds beef tenderloin, chopped

¼ cup heavy cream

1 teaspoon curry paste

¼ teaspoon minced garlic

1 teaspoon coconut oil, melted

1. Mix heavy cream with curry paste and minced garlic. 2. Then put the beef tenderloin in the curry mixture and leave for 10 minutes to marinate. 3. Place the Crisper Tray in the bottom position and spray it with oil. Add the food to it and close the lid. Move SmartSwitch to AIR FRY/STOVETOP, set the cooking temperature to 370°F and the cooking time to 30 minutes. 4. Serve and enjoy.

Per Serving: Calories 516; Fat: 24.18g; Sodium: 132mg; Carbs: 0.55g; Fiber: 0.3g; Sugar: 0.22g; Protein: 69.41g

Beef Meatballs

Prep Time: 5 minutes | Cook Time: 25 minutes | Serves: 4

2-pound ground beef

1 teaspoon dried rosemary

1 teaspoon onion powder

½ teaspoon salt

1 tablespoon olive oil

1. Mix ground beef with dried rosemary, onion powder, and salt. 2. Make the meatballs. 3. Place the Crisper Tray in the bottom position. Add the meatballs to it, spray them with oil and close the lid. Move SmartSwitch to AIR FRY/STOVETOP, set the cooking temperature to 360°F and the cooking time to 25 minutes. 4. Serve and enjoy.

Per Serving: Calories 517; Fat: 28.57g; Sodium: 430mg; Carbs: 0.51g; Fiber: 0.1g; Sugar: 0.04g; Protein: 60.44g

Basil Beef Steak

Prep Time: 10 minutes | Cook Time: 40 minutes | Serves: 4

3-pounds beef steak

2 tablespoons coconut oil, melted

1 tablespoon dried basil

½ teaspoon salt

1. Rub the beef steak with dried basil and salt. 2. Place the Crisper Tray in the bottom position. Add the steak to it, spray them with oil and close the lid. Move SmartSwitch to AIR FRY/STOVETOP, set the cooking temperature to 365°F and the cooking time to 40 minutes. 3. Flip the steak halfway through. 4. Serve and enjoy.

Per Serving: Calories 535; Fat: 25.55g; Sodium: 488mg; Carbs: 0.02g; Fiber: 0g; Sugar: 0g; Protein: 71.91g

Jalapeno Beef Casserole

Prep Time: 10 minutes | Cook Time: 40 minutes | Serves: 4

2 oz. Provolone cheese, grated

1 teaspoon coconut oil, softened

1 teaspoon dried cilantro

2-pounds ground beef

1 jalapeno pepper, sliced

1 teaspoon chili powder

¼ cup beef broth

1. Mix ground beef with dried cilantro, jalapeno pepper, and chili powder in a bowl. 2. Place the Crisper Tray in the bottom position and spray it with coconut oil. 3. Add the food to it and close the lid. Move SmartSwitch to AIR FRY/STOVETOP, set the cooking temperature to 360°F and the cooking time to 40 minutes. 4. Serve and enjoy.

Per Serving: Calories 553; Fat: 30.2g; Sodium: 302mg; Carbs: 2.17g; Fiber: 0.4g; Sugar: 0.27g; Protein: 64.22g

Garlic Beef Burgers

Prep Time: 15 minutes | Cook Time: 15 minutes | Serves: 4

2-pounds ground beef

1 teaspoon garlic powder

1 egg, beaten

1 teaspoon ground black pepper

1. Mix ground beef with garlic powder, ground black pepper, and egg. 2. Make the burgers from the mixture. 3. Place the Crisper Tray in the bottom position. Add the burgers to it and close the lid. Move SmartSwitch to AIR FRY/STOVETOP, set the cooking temperature to 385°F and the cooking time to 15 minutes. 4. Serve and enjoy.

Per Serving: Calories 505; Fat: 26.25g; Sodium: 155mg; Carbs: 1.11g; Fiber: 0.3g; Sugar: 0.06g; Protein: 61.96g

Artichoke & Beef Cubes

Prep Time: 10 minutes | Cook Time: 65 minutes | Serves: 4

1 and ½ pounds beef stew meat, cubed

6 oz. artichoke hearts, chopped

1 cup beef broth

1 teaspoon Italian seasonings

1 garlic clove, peeled

1 teaspoon ground nutmeg

1 teaspoon coconut oil

1. Mix all the ingredients in a bowl. 2. Place the Crisper Tray in the bottom position. Add the food to it and close the lid. Move SmartSwitch to AIR FRY/STOVETOP, set the cooking temperature to 350°F and the cooking time to 65 minutes. 3. Serve and enjoy.

Per Serving: Calories 158; Fat: 13.38g; Sodium: 545mg; Carbs: 8.33g; Fiber: 3.3g; Sugar: 2.15g; Protein: 2.54g

Beef Shank

Prep Time: 15 minutes | Cook Time: 40 minutes | Serves: 6

3-pound beef shank

¼ cup apple cider vinegar

1 tablespoon avocado oil

1 teaspoon white pepper

½ teaspoon salt

1. Mix avocado oil with apple cider vinegar, white pepper, and salt. 2. Sprinkle the beef shank with apple cider vinegar mixture. 3. Place the Crisper Tray in the bottom position. Add the beef shank to it and close the lid. Move SmartSwitch to AIR FRY/STOVETOP, set the cooking temperature to 365°F and the cooking time to 40 minutes. 4. Serve and enjoy.

Per Serving: Calories 317; Fat: 11.09g; Sodium: 337mg; Carbs: 1.44g; Fiber: 0.1g; Sugar: 0.99g; Protein: 49.38g

Chives Beef Sirloin

2 oz. chives, chopped

2-pound beef sirloin, chopped

3 tablespoons apple cider vinegar

1 tablespoon avocado oil

½ teaspoon minced garlic

1 teaspoon dried dill

1. Mix the beef sirloin with the remaining ingredients. 2. Place the Crisper Tray in the bottom position. Add the food to it and close the lid. Move SmartSwitch to AIR FRY/STOVETOP, set the cooking temperature to 365°F and the cooking time to 35 minutes. 3. Toss the food every 10 minutes. 4. Serve and enjoy.

Per Serving: Calories 468; Fat: 28.92g; Sodium: 121mg; Carbs: 1.13g; Fiber: 0.5g; Sugar: 0.31g; Protein: 47.47g

Herbed Beef Sirloin

1-pound beef sirloin

2 tablespoons avocado oil

1 teaspoon dried thyme

1 teaspoon coconut aminos

1. Mix beef sirloin with avocado oil, dried thyme, and coconut aminos. Marinate the beef sirloin for 10 minutes. 2. Place the Crisper Tray in the bottom position. Add the food to it and close the lid. Move SmartSwitch to AIR FRY/STOVETOP, set the cooking temperature to 360°F and the cooking time to 40 minutes. 3. Serve and enjoy.

Per Serving: Calories 277; Fat: 19.63g; Sodium: 61mg; Carbs: 0.1g; Fiber: 0g; Sugar: 0.03g; Protein: 23.47g

Marinated Beef Loin

Prep Time: 5 minutes | Cook Time: 75 minutes | Serves: 4

¼ cup apple cider vinegar

1 teaspoon dried rosemary

½ teaspoon ground coriander

1 garlic clove, crushed

1 tablespoon olive oil

2-pounds beef loin, roughly chopped

1. Mix all the ingredients in a bowl. 2. Place the Crisper Tray in the bottom position. Add the food to it and close the lid. Move SmartSwitch to AIR FRY/STOVETOP, set the cooking temperature to 355°F and the cooking time to 75 minutes. 3. Serve and enjoy.

Per Serving: Calories 546; Fat: 37.52g; Sodium: 119mg; Carbs: 2.04g; Fiber: 0.1g; Sugar: 1.5g; Protein: 46.77g

Lamb Steak

Prep Time: 10 minutes | Cook Time: 15 minutes | Serves: 2

14 oz. lamb steak

1 teaspoon ground coriander

1 teaspoon garlic powder

1 tablespoon olive oil

1. Rub the lamb steak with ground coriander, garlic powder, and olive oil. 2. Place the Crisper Tray in the bottom position. Add the lamb steak to it and close the lid. Move SmartSwitch to AIR FRY/STOVETOP, set the cooking temperature to 385°F and the cooking time to 12 minutes. 3. Flip the steak halfway through. 4. Serve and enjoy.

Per Serving: Calories 315; Fat: 15.97g; Sodium: 128mg; Carbs: 1.13g; Fiber: 0.1g; Sugar: 0.04g; Protein: 42.13g

Cauliflower Lamb Fritters

1 teaspoon onion powder	2-pound lamb, minced
1 teaspoon garlic powder	½ cup cauliflower, shredded
½ teaspoon ground coriander	Cooking spray
1 teaspoon salt	

1. Mix the onion powder with garlic powder, ground coriander, salt, lamb, and cauliflower in a bowl. Make the fritters from the beef mixture. 2. Place the Crisper Tray in the bottom position and spray it with cooking spray. Add the fritters to it and close the lid. Move SmartSwitch to AIR FRY/STOVETOP, set the cooking temperature to 360°F and the cooking time to 20 minutes. 3. Flip the fritters halfway through. 4. Serve and enjoy.

Per Serving: Calories 284; Fat: 19.1g; Sodium: 379mg; Carbs: 0.85g; Fiber: 0.2g; Sugar: 0.16g; Protein: 28.03g

Chapter 5 Fish and Seafood Recipes

Sea Bass Fillet with Tomato

Prep Time: 5 minutes | Cook Time: 16 minutes | Serves: 4

1½ pounds sea bass fillet

2 tablespoons lemon juice

2 garlic cloves, minced

½ cup coconut, shredded

½ cup all-purpose flour

Coarse sea salt and ground black pepper, to taste

2 tomatoes, sliced

1. Toss the fish fillets with the lemon juice, garlic, coconut, flour, salt, and black pepper. 2. Place the Crisper Tray in the bottom position. Add the food to it and close the lid. Move SmartSwitch to AIR FRY/STOVETOP, set the cooking temperature to 400°F and the cooking time to 16 minutes. 3. Flip the fillet and top them with tomatoes halfway through. 4. Serve and enjoy.

Per Serving: Calories 237; Fat: 3.68g; Sodium: 149mg; Carbs: 15.41g; Fiber: 1.1g; Sugar: 1.8g; Protein: 33.59g

Honey Garlic Trout

Prep Time: 5 minutes | Cook Time: 15 minutes | Serves: 4

1 pound trout, cut into sticks

1 tablespoon olive oil

2 tablespoons liquid honey

2 teaspoons apple cider vinegar

2 cloves garlic, minced

Sea salt and ground black pepper, to taste

½ teaspoon cayenne pepper

1. Toss all ingredients in a bowl. 2. Place the Crisper Tray in the bottom position. Add the food to it and close the lid. Move SmartSwitch to AIR FRY/STOVETOP, set the cooking temperature to 400°F and the cooking time to 12 minutes. Toss the food halfway through. 3. Serve and enjoy.

Per Serving: Calories 238; Fat: 10.94g; Sodium: 61mg; Carbs: 10.36g; Fiber: 0.3g; Sugar: 9.24g; Protein: 23.93g

Fried Shrimp

Prep Time: 5 minutes | Cook Time: 10 minutes | Serves: 4

½ cup flour	1 cup seasoned breadcrumbs
Sea salt and lemon pepper, to taste	2 tablespoons olive oil
2 large eggs	1 pound shrimp, peeled and deveined

1. Mix the flour, salt, and lemon pepper in a shallow bowl. 2. Beat the eggs in a second bowl, and place the breadcrumbs in a third bowl. 3. Dip the shrimp in the flour mixture, then in the whisked eggs; finally, roll the shrimp over the breadcrumbs until they are well coated on all sides. 4. Place the Crisper Tray in the bottom position. Add the shrimp to it, drizzle the olive oil over the shrimp and close the lid. Move SmartSwitch to AIR FRY/STOVETOP, set the cooking temperature to 400°F and the cooking time to 10 minutes. 5. Flip the food halfway through. 6. Serve and enjoy.

Per Serving: Calories 204; Fat: 6.76g; Sodium: 490mg; Carbs: 12.42g; Fiber: 1g; Sugar: 1.91g; Protein: 22.37g

Cod Patties

Prep Time: 5 minutes | Cook Time: 15 minutes | Serves: 4

1 pound cod fish, boneless and chopped	Sea salt and ground black pepper, to taste
½ cup breadcrumbs	½ teaspoon onion powder
2 medium eggs	1 teaspoon hot paprika
1 teaspoon Dijon mustard	1 tablespoon olive oil
2 garlic cloves, minced	4 hamburger buns

1. Mix all of the ingredients except for the hamburger buns in a bowl. 2. Shape the mixture into four patties. 3. Place the Crisper Tray in the bottom position. Add the patties to it and close the lid. Move SmartSwitch to AIR FRY/STOVETOP, set the cooking temperature to 400°F and the cooking time to 14 minutes. 4. Flip the patties halfway through. 5. Serve on hamburger buns and enjoy!

Per Serving: Calories 215; Fat: 6.89g; Sodium: 510mg; Carbs: 14.59g; Fiber: 1.2g; Sugar: 17.772.14g; Protein: 22.72g

Salmon Sticks

Prep Time: 5 minutes | Cook Time: 10 minutes | Serves: 4

1 egg, beaten

½ cup all-purpose flour

Sea salt and ground black pepper, to taste

1 teaspoon hot paprika

½ cup seasoned breadcrumbs

1 tablespoon olive oil

1 pound salmon strips

1. Thoroughly combine the egg, flour, and spices in a bowl. 2. In a separate bowl, thoroughly combine the breadcrumbs and olive oil. 3. Dip the salmon strips into the flour mixture to coat; roll the fish pieces over the breadcrumb mixture until they are well coated on all sides. 4. Place the Crisper Tray in the bottom position. Add the strips to it and close the lid. Move SmartSwitch to AIR FRY/STOVETOP, set the cooking temperature to 400°F and the cooking time to 10 minutes. 5. Flip the strips halfway through. 6. Serve and enjoy.

Per Serving: Calories 333; Fat: 12.78g; Sodium: 1739mg; Carbs: 22.25g; Fiber: 2.9g; Sugar: 1.99g; Protein: 27.24g

Tiger Prawns with Sherry Wine

Prep Time: 5 minutes | Cook Time: 10 minutes | Serves: 4

1½ pounds tiger prawns, peeled and deveined

1 tablespoon coconut oil

1 teaspoon garlic, crushed

1 teaspoon Old Bay seasoning

Coarse sea salt and ground black pepper, to taste

¼ cup sherry wine

1 teaspoon Dijon mustard

1. Toss all ingredients in a bowl. 2. Place the Crisper Tray in the bottom position. Add the prawns to it and close the lid. Move SmartSwitch to AIR FRY/STOVETOP, set the cooking temperature to 400°F and the cooking time to 9 minutes. 3. Toss the food halfway through. 4. Serve and enjoy.

Per Serving: Calories 62; Fat: 3.67g; Sodium: 19mg; Carbs: 7.82g; Fiber: 1.1g; Sugar: 3.59g; Protein: 1.51g

Sea Bass with Potato Scales

Prep Time: 10 minutes | Cook Time: 10 minutes | Serves: 2

2 (6- to 8-ounce) fillets of sea bass

Salt and freshly ground black pepper

¼ cup mayonnaise

2 teaspoons finely chopped lemon zest

1 teaspoon chopped fresh thyme

2 fingerling potatoes, very thinly sliced into rounds

Olive oil

½ clove garlic, crushed into a paste

1 tablespoon capers, drained and rinsed

1 tablespoon olive oil

1 teaspoon lemon juice, to taste

1. Season the fish well with salt and freshly ground black pepper. 2. Mix the mayonnaise, lemon zest and thyme together in a small bowl. 3. Spread a thin layer of the mayonnaise mixture on both fillets. 4. Start layering rows of potato slices onto the fish fillets to simulate the fish scales. The second row should overlap the first row slightly. 5. Dabbing a little more mayonnaise along the upper edge of the row of potatoes where the next row overlaps will help the potato slices stick. 6. Press the potatoes onto the fish to secure them well and season again with salt. Brush or spray the potato layer with olive oil. 7. Place the Crisper Tray in the bottom position. Add the fish to it and close the lid. Move SmartSwitch to AIR FRY/STOVETOP, set the cooking temperature to 400°F and the cooking time to 10 minutes. 8. While the fish is cooking, add the garlic, capers, olive oil and lemon juice to the remaining mayonnaise mixture to make the caper aïoli. 9. Serve the fish warm with a dollop of the aïoli on top or on the side.

Per Serving: Calories 570; Fat: 19.27g; Sodium: 443mg; Carbs: 66.5g; Fiber: 8.7g; Sugar: 3.35g; Protein: 33.22g

Tartar Sauce

Prep Time: 10 minutes | Cook Time: 0 minute | Serves: 2

1 cup mayonnaise

⅓ cup dill pickle relish

2 tablespoons capers, rinsed and chopped

1 tablespoon lemon juice

Dash cayenne pepper

Salt and freshly ground black pepper

1. Mix all the ingredients together in a bowl. 2. Season the sauce to taste with salt and freshly ground black pepper. 3. Serve the dish of your choice with the sauce.

Per Serving: Calories 443; Fat: 38.43g; Sodium: 1458mg; Carbs: 18.83g; Fiber: 2.1g; Sugar: 13.03g; Protein: 7.52g

Black Cod with Grapes

Prep Time: 10 minutes | Cook Time: 15 minutes | Serves: 2

2 (6- to 8-ounce) fillets of black cod (or sablefish)

Salt and freshly ground black pepper

Olive oil

1 cup grapes, halved

1 small bulb fennel, sliced ¼-inch thick

½ cup pecans

3 cups shredded kale

2 teaspoons white balsamic vinegar or white wine vinegar

2 tablespoons extra virgin olive oil

1. Season the cod fillets with salt and pepper and drizzle, brush or spray a little olive oil on top. 2. Place the Crisper Tray in the bottom position. Add the fillets to it with skin-side down and close the lid. Move SmartSwitch to AIR FRY/STOVETOP, set the cooking temperature to 400°F and the cooking time to 10 minutes. 3. Remove the fillets to a side plate and loosely tent with foil to rest. 4. Toss the grapes, fennel and pecans in a bowl with a drizzle of olive oil and season with salt and pepper. Add the grapes, fennel and pecans to the cooking pot and air-fry them for 5 minutes at 400°F, tossing them once during the cooking time. 5. Transfer the grapes, fennel and pecans to a bowl with the kale. 6. Dress the kale with the balsamic vinegar and olive oil, season to taste with salt and pepper and serve alongside the cooked fish.

Per Serving: Calories 548; Fat: 41.74g; Sodium: 255mg; Carbs: 27.82g; Fiber: 7.6g; Sugar: 17.83g; Protein: 20.56g

Barramundi with Mustard Crust

Prep Time: 5 minutes | Cook Time: 15 minutes | Serves: 4

1 pound Barramundi fillets

Sea salt and ground Szechuan pepper, to taste

1 tablespoon sesame oil

2 tablespoons rice wine vinegar

½ cup seasoned breadcrumbs

1 tablespoon grain mustard

1. Toss the fish with the remaining ingredients. 2. Place the Crisper Tray in the bottom position. Add the fillets to it and close the lid. Move SmartSwitch to AIR FRY/STOVETOP, set the cooking temperature to 400°F and the cooking time to 12 minutes. 3. Flip the fillets halfway through. 4. Serve and enjoy.

Per Serving: Calories 422; Fat: 23.96g; Sodium: 1832mg; Carbs: 21.44g; Fiber: 9.5g; Sugar: 3.37g; Protein: 27.23g

Breaded Fish Sticks with Tartar Sauce

Prep Time: 10 minutes | Cook Time: 6 minutes | Serves: 2-3

12 ounces cod or flounder

½ cup flour

½ teaspoon paprika

1 teaspoon salt

Lots of freshly ground black pepper

2 eggs, lightly beaten

1½ cups panko breadcrumbs

1 teaspoon salt

Vegetable oil

Tartar Sauce:

¼ cup mayonnaise

2 teaspoons lemon juice

2 tablespoons finely chopped sweet pickles

Salt and freshly ground black pepper

1. Cut the fish into ¾-inch wide sticks or strips. Set up a dredging station. 2. Combine the flour, paprika, salt and pepper in a shallow dish. 3. Beat the eggs lightly in a second shallow dish. Finally, mix the breadcrumbs and salt in a third shallow dish. 4. Coat the fish sticks by dipping the fish into the flour, then the egg and finally the breadcrumbs, coating on all sides in each step and pressing the crumbs firmly onto the fish. 5. Place the finished sticks on a plate or baking sheet while you finish all the sticks. 6. Place the Crisper Tray in the bottom position. Add the fish sticks to it, spray them with oil and close the lid. Move SmartSwitch to AIR FRY/STOVETOP, set the cooking temperature to 400°F and the cooking time to 6 minutes. 7. Flip the sticks after 4 minutes of cooking time. 8. While the fish is cooking, mix the tartar sauce ingredients together. 9. Serve the fish sticks warm with the tartar sauce and some French fries on the side.

Per Serving: Calories 523; Fat: 15.57g; Sodium: 2736mg; Carbs: 60.53g; Fiber: 3.5g; Sugar: 7.64g; Protein: 32.99g

Spicy Fish Street Tacos with Sriracha Slaw

Sriracha Slaw

½ cup mayonnaise

2 tablespoons rice vinegar

1 teaspoon sugar

2 tablespoons sriracha chili sauce

5 cups shredded green cabbage

¼ cup shredded carrots

2 scallions, chopped

Salt and freshly ground black pepper

Tacos

½ cup flour

1 teaspoon chili powder

½ teaspoon ground cumin

1 teaspoon salt

Freshly ground black pepper

½ teaspoon baking powder

1 egg, beaten

¼ cup milk

1 cup breadcrumbs

1 pound mahi-mahi or snapper fillets

1 tablespoon canola or vegetable oil

6 (6-inch) flour tortillas

1 lime, cut into wedges

1. Combine the mayonnaise, rice vinegar, sugar, and sriracha sauce in a large bowl; add the green cabbage, carrots, and scallions. Toss them until all the vegetables are coated with the dressing and season with salt and pepper. 2. Refrigerate the slaw until you are ready to serve the tacos. 3. Combine the flour, chili powder, cumin, salt, pepper and baking powder in a bowl. Add the egg and milk and mix until the batter is smooth. Place the breadcrumbs in shallow dish. 4. Cut the fish fillets into 1-inch wide sticks, approximately 4-inches long. 5. Dip the fish sticks into the batter, coating all sides. 6. Let the excess batter drip off the fish and then roll them in the breadcrumbs, patting the crumbs onto all sides of the fish sticks. 7. Set the coated fish on a plate or baking sheet until all the fish has been coated. 8. Spray the coated fish sticks with oil on all sides. 9. Place the Crisper Tray in the bottom position. Add the fish sticks to it and close the lid. Move SmartSwitch to AIR FRY/STOVETOP, set the cooking temperature to 400°F and the cooking time to 5 minutes. 10. Flip the fish sticks halfway through. 11. While the fish is air-frying, warm the tortilla shells either in a skillet with a little oil over medium-high heat for a couple minutes. 12. Fold the tortillas in half and keep them warm until the remaining tortillas and fish are ready. 13. To assemble the tacos, place two pieces of the fish in each tortilla shell and top with the sriracha slaw. 14. Squeeze the lime wedge over top and dig in.

Per Serving: Calories 949; Fat: 31.45g; Sodium: 2382mg; Carbs: 110.43g; Fiber: 9.7g; Sugar: 15.73g; Protein: 54.36g

Fish and "Chips"

½ cup flour

½ teaspoon paprika

¼ teaspoon ground white pepper (or freshly ground black pepper)

1 egg

¼ cup mayonnaise

2 cups salt & vinegar kettle cooked potato chips, coarsely crushed

12 ounces cod

Lemon wedges

Tartar sauce

1. Combine the flour, paprika and pepper in a shallow dish. Combine the egg and mayonnaise in a second shallow dish. Place the crushed potato chips in a third shallow dish. 2. Cut the cod into 6 pieces. Dredge each piece of fish in the flour, then dip it into the egg mixture and then place it into the crushed potato chips. Make sure all sides of the fish are covered and pat the chips gently onto the fish so they stick well. 3. Place the Crisper Tray in the bottom position. Add the fillets to it and close the lid. Move SmartSwitch to AIR FRY/STOVETOP, set the cooking temperature to 370°F and the cooking time to 10 minutes. 4. Flip the fillets halfway through. 5. Transfer the fish to a platter and serve with tartar sauce and lemon wedges.

Per Serving: Calories 269; Fat: 10.35g; Sodium: 575mg; Carbs: 18.7g; Fiber: 1.1g; Sugar: 1.13g; Protein: 23.87g

Cheese Monkfish Fillets

1 pound monkfish fillets

Coarse sea salt and ground black pepper, to taste

2 tablespoons butter

2 tablespoons lemon juice

4 tablespoon Parmesan cheese, grated

1. Toss the fish fillets with the remaining ingredients, except for the Parmesan cheese. 2. Place the Crisper Tray in the bottom position. Add the fillets to it and close the lid. Move SmartSwitch to AIR FRY/STOVETOP, set the cooking temperature to 400°F and the cooking time to 14 minutes. Flip the fillets halfway through. 3. Top the fish fillets with the grated Parmesan cheese and serve immediately.

Per Serving: Calories 403; Fat: 27.58g; Sodium: 692mg; Carbs: 11.45g; Fiber: 6.9g; Sugar: 1.11g; Protein: 27.59g

Maple-Glazed Salmon

4 (6-ounce) fillets of salmon

Salt and freshly ground black pepper

Vegetable oil

¼ cup pure maple syrup

3 tablespoons balsamic vinegar

1 teaspoon Dijon mustard

1. Season the salmon well with salt and freshly ground black pepper. 2. Place the Crisper Tray in the bottom position and spray it with oil. Add the fillets to it and close the lid. Move SmartSwitch to AIR FRY/STOVETOP, set the cooking temperature to 400°F and the cooking time to 5 minutes. 3. While the salmon fillets are air-frying, combine the maple syrup, balsamic vinegar and Dijon mustard in a small saucepan over medium heat and stir to blend well. Let the mixture simmer until lightly thickened while the fish is cooking. 4. Brush the glaze on the salmon fillets and air-fry for an additional 5 minutes. 5. The salmon should feel firm to the touch when finished and the glaze should be nicely browned on top. 6. Brush a little more glaze on top before removing and serving with rice and vegetables, or a nice green salad.

Per Serving: Calories 538; Fat: 14.98g; Sodium: 217mg; Carbs: 15.34g; Fiber: 0.1g; Sugar: 13.72g; Protein: 79.87g

Sherry Sauce

2 tablespoons butter, divided

1 shallot, minced

½ cup dry sherry

½ cup heavy cream

1 teaspoon Dijon mustard

Salt and freshly ground black pepper

½ teaspoon chopped fresh tarragon

1. Melt one tablespoon of butter in a small saucepan over medium heat. 2. Sauté the shallot until it just starts to brown. Pour in the sherry and scrape up any brown bits on the bottom of the pan. 3. Simmer them until the liquid has reduced by half. 4. Add the heavy cream and Dijon mustard and continue to simmer until the sauce thickens. Season to taste with salt and freshly ground black pepper. 5. If you want a very smooth sauce, strain the sauce through a fine strainer before proceeding. Otherwise, just stir in the remaining butter and tarragon and serve.

Per Serving: Calories 263; Fat: 22.79g; Sodium: 150mg; Carbs: 16.07g; Fiber: 2.1g; Sugar: 13.56g; Protein: 1.19g

Large Shrimp with Amaretto Glaze

Prep Time: 10 minutes | Cook Time: 10 minutes | Serves: 10-12

1 cup flour

½ teaspoon baking powder

1 teaspoon salt

2 eggs, beaten

½ cup milk

2 tablespoons olive or vegetable oil

2 cups sliced almonds

2 pounds large shrimp (about 32 to 40 shrimp), peeled and deveined, tails left on

2 cups amaretto liqueur

1. Combine the flour, baking powder and salt in a large bowl. Add the eggs, milk and oil and stir until it forms a smooth batter. Coarsely crush the sliced almonds into a second shallow dish with your hands. 2. Dry the shrimp well with paper towels. Dip the shrimp into the batter and shake off any excess batter, leaving just enough to lightly coat the shrimp. 3. Transfer the shrimp to the dish with the almonds and coat completely. 4. Place the coated shrimp on a plate and when all the shrimp have been coated, freeze the shrimp for 1 hour. 5. Place the Crisper Tray in the bottom position. Add the shrimp to it and close the lid. Move SmartSwitch to AIR FRY/ STOVETOP, set the cooking temperature to 400°F and the cooking time to 10 minutes. 6. Flip the shrimp halfway through. You can cook them in batches. 7. While the shrimp are cooking, bring the Amaretto to a boil in a small saucepan on the stovetop. Lower the heat and simmer for 10 minutes until it has reduced and thickened into a glaze. 8. Brush the shrimp with the warm amaretto glaze. Serve warm.

Per Serving: Calories 297; Fat: 5.29g; Sodium: 647mg; Carbs: 31.15g; Fiber: 0.3g; Sugar: 18.43g; Protein: 13.27g

Lemon-Dill Mayonnaise

Prep Time: 10 minutes | Cook Time: 0 minute | Serves: 2

¼ cup mayonnaise

1 teaspoon lemon juice

1 teaspoon lemon zest

2 tablespoons finely chopped dill weed

Salt and freshly ground black pepper

1. Mix all the ingredients together in a bowl and spread the mixture on the buns before serving. 2. Serve the dish you like with the sauce.

Per Serving: Calories 106; Fat: 9.69g; Sodium: 238mg; Carbs: 3.03g; Fiber: 0.8g; Sugar: 0.38g; Protein: 2.43g

Lemon Salmon Burgers

Prep Time: 10 minutes | Cook Time: 10 minutes | Serves: 4

2 (6-ounce) fillets of salmon, finely chopped by hand or in a food processor

1 cup fine breadcrumbs

1 teaspoon freshly grated lemon zest

2 tablespoons chopped fresh dill weed

1 teaspoon salt

Freshly ground black pepper

2 eggs, lightly beaten

4 brioche or hamburger buns

Lettuce, tomato, red onion, avocado, mayonnaise or mustard, to serve

1. Combine all the ingredients in a bowl. Form 4 balls from the mixture. Flatten the balls into patties, making an indentation in the center of each patty with your thumb and flattening the sides of the burgers. 2. Place the Crisper Tray in the bottom position. Add the burgers to it and close the lid. Move SmartSwitch to AIR FRY/STOVETOP, set the cooking temperature to 400°F and the cooking time to 8 minutes. 3. Flip the burgers halfway through. 4. Serve the burgers on soft brioche buns with your choice of topping – lettuce, tomato, red onion, avocado, mayonnaise or mustard.

Per Serving: Calories 579; Fat: 20.96g; Sodium: 1323mg; Carbs: 38.87g; Fiber: 2.6g; Sugar: 6.19g; Protein: 56.12g

Cajun Shrimp

Prep Time: 5 minutes | Cook Time: 10 minutes | Serves: 2

12 ounces uncooked medium shrimp, peeled and deveined

1 teaspoon cayenne pepper

1 teaspoon Old Bay seasoning

½ teaspoon smoked paprika

2 tablespoons olive oil

1 teaspoon salt

1. Combine the shrimp, cayenne pepper, Old Bay, paprika, olive oil, and salt in a medium bowl. 2. Toss the shrimp in the oil and spices until the shrimp is thoroughly coated with both. 3. Place the Crisper Tray in the bottom position. Add the shrimp to it and close the lid. Move SmartSwitch to AIR FRY/STOVETOP, set the cooking temperature to 390°F and the cooking time to 6 minutes. 4. Toss the food halfway through. 5. Serve and enjoy.

Per Serving: Calories 246; Fat: 15.48g; Sodium: 2127mg; Carbs: 2.61g; Fiber: 0.5g; Sugar: 0.16g; Protein: 23.37g

Crab Cakes

1 teaspoon butter

⅓ cup finely diced onion

⅓ cup finely diced celery

¼ cup mayonnaise

1 teaspoon Dijon mustard

1 egg

Pinch ground cayenne pepper

1 teaspoon salt

Freshly ground black pepper

16 ounces lump crabmeat

½ cup + 2 tablespoons panko breadcrumbs, divided

1. Melt the butter in a skillet over medium heat. Sauté the onion and celery for 4 minutes until it starts to soften. 2. Transfer the cooked vegetables to a large bowl. Add the mayonnaise, Dijon mustard, egg, cayenne pepper, salt and freshly ground black pepper to the bowl. Gently fold in the lump crabmeat and 2 tablespoons of panko breadcrumbs. Stir carefully so you don't break up all the crab pieces. 3. Place the remaining panko breadcrumbs in a shallow dish. 4. Divide the crab mixture into 4 portions and shape each portion into a round patty. 5. Dredge the crab patties in the breadcrumbs, coating both sides as well as the edges with the crumbs. 6. Place the Crisper Tray in the bottom position. Add the crab cakes to it and close the lid. Move SmartSwitch to AIR FRY/STOVETOP, set the cooking temperature to 400°F and the cooking time to 10 minutes. 7. Flip the food halfway through. 8. Serve the crab cakes with tartar sauce or cocktail sauce, or dress it up with the suggestion below.

Per Serving: Calories 454; Fat: 11.59g; Sodium: 763mg; Carbs: 46.44g; Fiber: 20.5g; Sugar: 1.39g; Protein: 46.79g

Chimichurri Squid

1½ pounds small squid tubes

Sea salt and ground black pepper, to taste

1 teaspoon paprika

½ cup parsley, minced

2 cloves garlic, minced

¼ cup olive oil

1. Toss the squid, salt, black pepper, and paprika in a bowl. 2. Place the Crisper Tray in the bottom position. Add the food to it and close the lid. Move SmartSwitch to AIR FRY/STOVETOP, set the cooking temperature to 400°F and the cooking time to 5 minutes. 3. Toss the food halfway through. 4. Serve and enjoy.

Per Serving: Calories 287; Fat: 16.01g; Sodium: 81mg; Carbs: 7.58g; Fiber: 0.6g; Sugar: 0.71g; Protein: 27.13g

Lobster Tails

2 tablespoons unsalted butter, melted

1 tablespoon minced garlic

1 teaspoon salt

1 tablespoon minced fresh chives

2 (4- to 6-ounce) frozen lobster tails

1. Combine the butter, garlic, salt, and chives in a bowl. 2. Butterfly the lobster tail: Starting at the meaty end of the tail, use kitchen shears to cut down the center of the top shell. Stop when you reach the fanned, wide part of the tail. 3. Carefully spread apart the meat and the shell along the cut line, but keep the meat attached where it connects to the wide part of the tail. 4. Gently disconnect the meat from the bottom of the shell. Lift the meat up and out of the shell. Close the shell under the meat, so the meat rests on top of the shell. 5. Place the Crisper Tray in the bottom position. Add the lobster tails to it and close the lid. Move SmartSwitch to AIR FRY/STOVETOP, set the cooking temperature to 380°F and the cooking time to 8 minutes. 6. Flip the lobster tails and brush them with more butter mixture halfway through. 7. The meat should be opaque when cooked. 8. Serve and enjoy.

Per Serving: Calories 132; Fat: 9.31g; Sodium: 1196mg; Carbs: 10.87g; Fiber: 0.1g; Sugar: 8.74g; Protein: 2.09g

Calamari in Beer

2 cups all-purpose flour

1 cup beer

Sea salt and ground black pepper, to taste

2 teaspoons garlic powder

1 teaspoon dried parsley flakes

1 tablespoon olive oil

1 pound calamari rings

1. Thoroughly combine the flour, beer, spices, and olive oil in a bowl. 2. Dip the calamari into the flour mixture to coat. 3. Place the Crisper Tray in the bottom position. Add the calamari to it and close the lid. Move SmartSwitch to AIR FRY/STOVETOP, set the cooking temperature to 400°F and the cooking time to 5 minutes. 4. Flip the food halfway through. 5. Serve and enjoy.

Per Serving: Calories 698; Fat: 29.67g; Sodium: 605mg; Carbs: 92.06g; Fiber: 4.7g; Sugar: 7.08g; Protein: 15.59g

Crab Cake Sliders

Prep Time: 5 minutes | Cook Time: 10 minutes | Serves: 4

1 pound crabmeat, shredded

¼ cup bread crumbs

2 teaspoons dried parsley

1 teaspoon salt

½ teaspoon freshly ground black pepper

1 large egg

2 tablespoons mayonnaise

1 teaspoon dry mustard

4 slider buns

Sliced tomato, lettuce leaves, and rémoulade sauce, for topping

1. Spray the air fryer basket with olive oil or spray an air fryer–size baking sheet with olive oil or cooking spray.

2. In a medium mixing bowl, combine the crabmeat, bread crumbs, parsley, salt, pepper, egg, mayonnaise, and dry mustard. 3. Form the crab mixture into 4 equal patties. 4. Place the Crisper Tray in the bottom position and spray it with oil. Add the crab cakes to it and close the lid. Move SmartSwitch to AIR FRY/STOVETOP, set the cooking temperature to 400°F and the cooking time to 10 minutes. 5. Flip the crab cakes halfway through. 6. Serve on slider buns with sliced tomato, lettuce, and rémoulade sauce.

Per Serving: Calories 810; Fat: 51.94g; Sodium: 2788mg; Carbs: 37.23g; Fiber: 1.1g; Sugar: 17.96g; Protein: 47.24g

Chapter 6 Snack and Appetizer Recipes

Cauliflower Rice

Prep Time: 5 minutes | Cook Time: 20 minutes | Serves: 4

3 cups cauliflower, shredded

1 tablespoon coconut oil

1 teaspoon ground turmeric

½ teaspoon dried oregano

1. Mix cauliflower with ground turmeric and dried oregano. 2. Place the Crisper Tray in the bottom position and spray it with coconut oil. Add the food to it and close the lid. Move SmartSwitch to AIR FRY/STOVETOP, set the cooking temperature to 360°F and the cooking time to 20 minutes. 3. Toss the rice from time to time to avoid burning. 4. Serve and enjoy.

Per Serving: Calories 52; Fat: 3.65g; Sodium: 24mg; Carbs: 4.58g; Fiber: 1.8g; Sugar: 1.56g; Protein: 1.62g

Cheese Portobello Patties

Prep Time: 10 minutes | Cook Time: 10 minutes | Serves: 4

10 oz. Portobello mushrooms, diced

1 egg, beaten

3 oz. Monterey Jack cheese, shredded

1 teaspoon dried cilantro

½ teaspoon white pepper

1 teaspoon avocado oil

2 tablespoons coconut flour

1. Mix mushrooms with egg, Monterey Jack cheese, cilantro, white pepper, and coconut flour in a bowl. 2. Make the patties from the mushroom mixture. 3. Place the Crisper Tray in the bottom position. Add the patties to it and close the lid. Move SmartSwitch to AIR FRY/STOVETOP, set the cooking temperature to 375°F and the cooking time to 8 minutes. 4. Flip the patties halfway through. 5. Serve and enjoy.

Per Serving: Calories 317; Fat: 9.34g; Sodium: 160mg; Carbs: 54.13g; Fiber: 8.3g; Sugar: 1.91g; Protein: 13.47g

Chopped Cauliflower

Prep Time: 15 minutes | Cook Time: 20 minutes | Serves: 2

1 cup cauliflower, chopped

2 eggs, beaten

½ cup Cheddar cheese, shredded

½ teaspoon chili powder

1 teaspoon coconut oil

½ cup heavy cream

1. Grease a suitable baking pan with coconut oil. 2. Mix the cauliflower with eggs, Cheddar cheese, chili powder, and heavy cream in a bowl. 3. Transfer the mixture in the prepared baking pan and flatten gently. 4. Place the Crisper Tray in the bottom position. Place the pan on the tray and close the lid. Move SmartSwitch to AIR FRY/ STOVETOP, and then use the center front arrows to select BAKE/ROAST. Set the cooking temperature to 385°F and the cooking time to 20 minutes. 5. Serve and enjoy.

Per Serving: Calories 402; Fat: 34.4g; Sodium: 362mg; Carbs: 5.3g; Fiber: 1.3g; Sugar: 2.65g; Protein: 18.64g

Cilantro Tofu Cubes

Prep Time: 15 minutes | Cook Time: 10 minutes | Serves: 2

10 oz. tofu, cubed

1 teaspoon avocado oil

1 teaspoon dried cilantro

½ teaspoon ground paprika

½ teaspoon ground black pepper

1 tablespoon apple cider vinegar

1. Mix avocado oil with dried cilantro, ground paprika, ground black pepper, and apple cider vinegar in a bowl. 2. Mix the cubed tofu with avocado oil mixture and leave for 10 minutes to marinate. 3. Place the Crisper Tray in the bottom position. Add the tofu cubes to it and close the lid. Move SmartSwitch to AIR FRY/STOVETOP, set the cooking temperature to 385°F and the cooking time to 8 minutes. 4. Flip the food halfway through. 5. Serve and enjoy.

Per Serving: Calories 412; Fat: 30.96g; Sodium: 24mg; Carbs: 16.33g; Fiber: 5.9g; Sugar: 4.52g; Protein: 24.68g

Brussels Sprouts

Prep Time: 10 minutes | Cook Time: 20 minutes | Serves: 4

1 pound Brussels sprouts, trimmed and halved

1 tablespoon garlic powder

1 tablespoon coconut oil

½ teaspoon ground black pepper

1. Mix Brussel sprouts with garlic powder, coconut oil, and ground black pepper in a bowl. 2. Place the Crisper Tray in the bottom position. Add the food to it and close the lid. Move SmartSwitch to AIR FRY/STOVETOP, set the cooking temperature to 375°F and the cooking time to 20 minutes. 3. Toss the vegetables halfway through. 4. Serve and enjoy.

Per Serving: Calories 87; Fat: 3.77g; Sodium: 30mg; Carbs: 12.1g; Fiber: 4.6g; Sugar: 2.56g; Protein: 4.27g

Cheddar Zucchini Balls

Prep Time: 15 minutes | Cook Time: 10 minutes | Serves: 4

1 zucchini, grated

½ cup Cheddar cheese, shredded

1 egg, beaten

1 teaspoon chili powder

1 teaspoon avocado oil

1. Mix the zucchini with cheese, egg, and chili powder in a bowl. 2. Make the balls from the zucchini mixture. Sprinkle the zucchini balls with avocado oil. 3. Place the Crisper Tray in the bottom position. Add the zucchini balls to it and close the lid. Move SmartSwitch to AIR FRY/STOVETOP, set the cooking temperature to 385°F and the cooking time to 6 minutes. 4. Serve and enjoy.

Per Serving: Calories 95; Fat: 7.86g; Sodium: 141mg; Carbs: 0.72g; Fiber: 0.3g; Sugar: 0.14g; Protein: 5.51g

Mustard Cauliflower & Broccoli

Prep Time: 10 minutes | Cook Time: 20 minutes | Serves: 4

1 cup cauliflower, chopped

1 cup broccoli, chopped

1 tablespoon mustard

1 tablespoon avocado oil

1 teaspoon chili powder

½ teaspoon dried dill

1 teaspoon apple cider vinegar

1. Mix mustard with avocado oil, chili powder, dried dill, and apple cider vinegar in a bowl. 2. Place the Crisper Tray in the bottom position. Add the vegetables to it and close the lid. Move SmartSwitch to AIR FRY/ STOVETOP, set the cooking temperature to 385°F and the cooking time to 20 minutes. 3. Flip the vegetables halfway through. 4. Serve and enjoy.

Per Serving: Calories 45; Fat: 3.89g; Sodium: 74mg; Carbs: 2.34g; Fiber: 1.3g; Sugar: 0.64g; Protein: 1.11g

Egg Mushroom Fritters

Prep Time: 10 minutes | Cook Time: 6 minutes | Serves: 2

1 cup mushrooms, grinded

1 teaspoon garlic powder

1 egg, beaten

3 teaspoons coconut flour

½ teaspoon chili powder

1 teaspoon coconut oil

1 tablespoon almond flour

1. Mix the mushrooms with garlic powder, egg, coconut flour, chili powder, and almond flour in a bowl. 2. Make the mushroom fritters from the mixture. 3. Place the Crisper Tray in the bottom position and spray it with coconut oil. Add the food to it and close the lid. Move SmartSwitch to AIR FRY/STOVETOP, set the cooking temperature to 400°F and the cooking time to 6 minutes. 4. Flip the fritters halfway through. 5. Serve and enjoy.

Per Serving: Calories 73; Fat: 4.93g; Sodium: 63mg; Carbs: 3.61g; Fiber: 1g; Sugar: 1.34g; Protein: 4.78g

Keto Mushroom Risotto

Prep Time: 5 minutes | Cook Time: 20 minutes | Serves: 4

1 pound mushrooms, diced

¼ cup Cheddar cheese, shredded

3 cups cauliflower, shredded

1 cup beef broth

1 teaspoon dried oregano

1 teaspoon dried cilantro

1 tablespoon coconut oil

1. Mix all the ingredients in a bowl. 2. Place the Crisper Tray in the bottom position. Add the food to it and close the lid. Move SmartSwitch to AIR FRY/STOVETOP, set the cooking temperature to 375°F and the cooking time to 20 minutes. 3. Stir the risotto every 5 minutes to avoid burning. 4. Serve and enjoy.

Per Serving: Calories 138; Fat: 9.29g; Sodium: 237mg; Carbs: 9.21g; Fiber: 3.2g; Sugar: 4.43g; Protein: 7.76g

Cheddar Broccoli Tots

Prep Time: 15 minutes | Cook Time: 10 minutes | Serves: 4

1 teaspoon mascarpone

5 oz. Cheddar cheese, shredded

3 cups broccoli, chopped, boiled

¼ teaspoon onion powder

1 teaspoon avocado oil

1. Mix the mascarpone with Cheddar cheese, broccoli, and onion powder in a bowl. 2. Make the broccoli tots from the mixture. 3. Place the Crisper Tray in the bottom position. Add the food to it and close the lid. Move SmartSwitch to AIR FRY/STOVETOP, set the cooking temperature to 400°F and the cooking time to 8 minutes. 4. Serve and enjoy.

Per Serving: Calories 79; Fat: 4.42g; Sodium: 401mg; Carbs: 4.77g; Fiber: 0.8g; Sugar: 2.63g; Protein: 5.72g

Chives and Spinach Chops

Prep Time: 5 minutes | Cook Time: 10 minutes | Serves: 4

3 cups spinach, chopped

1 oz. chives, chopped

½ cup heavy cream

1 teaspoon chili powder

1. Mix spinach with chives, heavy cream, and chili powder. 2. Place the Crisper Tray in the bottom position. Add the mixture to it and close the lid. Move SmartSwitch to AIR FRY/STOVETOP, set the cooking temperature to 360°F and the cooking time to 10 minutes. 3. Carefully mix the meal before serving.

Per Serving: Calories 61; Fat: 5.79; Sodium: 43mg; Carbs: 1.88g; Fiber: 0.9g; Sugar: 0.69g; Protein: 1.27g

Zucchini Tots

Prep Time: 10 minutes | Cook Time: 15 minutes | Serves: 4

3 zucchinis, grated

½ cup coconut flour

2 eggs, beaten

1 teaspoon chili flakes

1 teaspoon salt

1 teaspoon avocado oil

1. Mix up grated carrot, salt, ground cumin, zucchini, Provolone cheese, chili flakes, egg, and coconut flour in a bowl. Stir the mass with the help of the spoon and make the small balls. 2. Place the Crisper Tray in the bottom position and spray it with oil. Add the food to it and close the lid. Move SmartSwitch to AIR FRY/STOVETOP, set the cooking temperature to 375°F and the cooking time to 12 minutes. 3. Toss the balls every 2 minutes to avoid burning. 4. Serve and enjoy.

Per Serving: Calories 51; Fat: 3.41g; Sodium: 664mg; Carbs: 1.86g; Fiber: 0.7g; Sugar: 0.91g; Protein: 3.29g

Egg Broccoli Hash Brown

Prep Time: 5 minutes | Cook Time: 15 minutes | Serves: 4

2 cups broccoli, chopped

3 eggs, whisked

1 tablespoon coconut oil

1 teaspoon dried oregano

1. Mix broccoli with eggs. 2. Place the Crisper Tray in the bottom position. Add the mixture and dried oregano to it, then spray them with oil and close the lid. Move SmartSwitch to AIR FRY/STOVETOP, set the cooking temperature to 350°F and the cooking time to 15 minutes. 3. Stir the meal every 5 minutes. 4. Serve and enjoy.

Per Serving: Calories 82; Fat: 6.65g; Sodium: 54mg; Carbs: 0.98g; Fiber: 0.6g; Sugar: 0.21g; Protein: 4.8g

Eggplant Bites

Prep Time: 10 minutes | Cook Time: 10 minutes | Serves: 5

2 medium eggplants, trimmed, sliced

4 oz. Parmesan, grated

1 teaspoon coconut oil, melted

1. Place the Crisper Tray in the bottom position and spray it with coconut oil. 2. Add the eggplant slices to it, top them with Parmesan cheese, and close the lid. Move SmartSwitch to AIR FRY/STOVETOP, set the cooking temperature to 390°F and the cooking time to 10 minutes. 3. Serve and enjoy.

Per Serving: Calories 146; Fat: 2.43g; Sodium: 265mg; Carbs: 21.96g; Fiber: 6.6g; Sugar: 8.08g; Protein: 11.22g

Cream Broccoli Puree

Prep Time: 10 minutes | Cook Time: 20 minutes | Serves: 4

1-pound broccoli, chopped

1 tablespoon coconut oil

¼ cup heavy cream

1 teaspoon salt

1. Place the Crisper Tray in the bottom position and spray it with oil. Add broccoli, heavy cream, and salt to it and close the lid. Move SmartSwitch to AIR FRY/STOVETOP, set the cooking temperature to 365°F and the cooking time to 20 minutes. 2. Mash the cooked broccoli mixture until you get the soft puree.

Per Serving: Calories 80; Fat: 6.73g; Sodium: 622mg; Carbs: 3.44g; Fiber: 3.1g; Sugar: 0.64g; Protein: 3.75g

Seasoned Brussel Sprouts

Prep Time: 10 minutes | Cook Time: 15 minutes | Serves: 6

1-pound Brussel sprouts

1 teaspoon garlic powder

1 teaspoon ground coriander

1 tablespoon coconut oil

1 tablespoon apple cider vinegar

1. Place the Crisper Tray in the bottom position and spray it with oil. Add Brussel sprouts, garlic powder, ground coriander, and apple cider vinegar to it and close the lid. Move SmartSwitch to AIR FRY/STOVETOP, set the cooking temperature to 390°F and the cooking time to 13 minutes. 2. Toss the Brussel sprouts from time to time to avoid burning. 3. Serve and enjoy.

Per Serving: Calories 54; Fat: 2.5g; Sodium: 19mg; Carbs: 7.17g; Fiber: 2.9g; Sugar: 1.69g; Protein: 2.64g

Coriander Fennel Wedges

Prep Time: 5 minutes | Cook Time: 15 minutes | Serves: 4

1 pound fennel bulb, cut into small wedges

1 teaspoon ground coriander

1 tablespoon avocado oil

½ teaspoon salt

1. Rub the fennel bulb with ground coriander, avocado oil, and salt. 2. Place the Crisper Tray in the bottom position. Add the fennel bulb to it and close the lid. Move SmartSwitch to AIR FRY/STOVETOP, set the cooking temperature to 390°F and the cooking time to 15 minutes. 3. Flip the food halfway through. 4. Serve and enjoy.

Per Serving: Calories 66; Fat: 3.73g; Sodium: 350mg; Carbs: 8.28g; Fiber: 3.5g; Sugar: 4.46g; Protein: 1.41g

Turmeric Tempeh

Prep Time: 10 minutes | Cook Time: 15 minutes | Serves: 4

1 teaspoon apple cider vinegar

1 tablespoon avocado oil

¼ teaspoon ground turmeric

6 oz. tempeh, chopped

1. Mix avocado oil with apple cider vinegar and ground turmeric. 2. Sprinkle the tempeh with turmeric mixture. 3. Place the Crisper Tray in the bottom position. Add the food to it and close the lid. Move SmartSwitch to AIR FRY/ STOVETOP, set the cooking temperature to 350°F and the cooking time to 12 minutes. Flip the food halfway through. 4. Serve and enjoy.

Per Serving: Calories 114; Fat: 8.1g; Sodium: 4mg; Carbs: 4.14g; Fiber: 0g; Sugar: 0.01g; Protein: 7.9g

Cheese Banana Peppers Mix

8 oz. banana peppers, chopped

1 tablespoon avocado oil

1 tablespoon dried oregano

2 tablespoons mascarpone

1 cup Monterey Jack cheese, shredded

1. Brush a suitable baking pan with avocado oil. 2. Mix banana peppers with dried oregano and mascarpone and put in the prepared baking pan. Top the peppers with Monterey Jack cheese. 3. Place the Crisper Tray in the bottom position. Place the pan on the tray and close the lid. Move SmartSwitch to AIR FRY/STOVETOP, and then use the center front arrows to select BAKE/ROAST. Set the cooking temperature to 365°F and the cooking time to 20 minutes. 4. Serve and enjoy.

Per Serving: Calories 177; Fat: 13.61g; Sodium: 202mg; Carbs: 5.59g; Fiber: 0.9g; Sugar: 3.06g; Protein: 9.21g

Keto Cauliflower Chops

2 cups cauliflower, chopped

1 oz. Parmesan, grated

1 tablespoon avocado oil

1. Sprinkle the cauliflower with avocado oil. 2. Place the Crisper Tray in the bottom position. Add the food to it and close the lid. Move SmartSwitch to AIR FRY/STOVETOP, set the cooking temperature to 390°F and the cooking time to 20 minutes. 3. Toss the cauliflower and sprinkle them with Parmesan cheese halfway through. 4. Serve and enjoy.

Per Serving: Calories 141; Fat: 8.01g; Sodium: 195mg; Carbs: 11g; Fiber: 2.1g; Sugar: 2.26g; Protein: 7.73g

Keto Cabbage Coleslaw

Prep Time: 10 minutes | Cook Time: 20 minutes | Serves: 4

1 cup white cabbage, shredded

2 tablespoons apple cider vinegar

½ cup heavy cream

1 teaspoon ground black pepper

1 tablespoon Dijon mustard

1. Mix white cabbage with heavy cream. 2. Place the Crisper Tray in the bottom position. Add the cabbage to it and close the lid. Move SmartSwitch to AIR FRY/STOVETOP, set the cooking temperature to 350°F and the cooking time to 20 minutes. 3. Stir the food from time to time. 4. Transfer the white cabbage mixture in the salad bowl. 5. Add all remaining ingredients and carefully mix. Enjoy.

Per Serving: Calories 64; Fat: 5.74g; Sodium: 55mg; Carbs: 2.82g; Fiber: 0.8g; Sugar: 1.34g; Protein: 0.85g

Brussel Sprouts with Coconut Shred

Prep Time: 10 minutes | Cook Time: 15 minutes | Serves: 4

8 oz. Brussels sprouts

1 tablespoon coconut shred

1 tablespoon coconut oil

1 teaspoon ground paprika

1 teaspoon ground black pepper

1. Mix all of the ingredients in a bowl. 2. Place the Crisper Tray in the bottom position. Add the food to it and close the lid. Move SmartSwitch to AIR FRY/STOVETOP, set the cooking temperature to 380°F and the cooking time to 15 minutes. 3. Toss the meal while cooking every 5 minutes. 4. Serve and enjoy.

Per Serving: Calories 57; Fat: 3.67g; Sodium: 19mg; Carbs: 5.89g; Fiber: 2.5g; Sugar: 1.41g; Protein: 2.08g

Chapter 7 Dessert Recipes

Apple Pies

Prep Time: 15 minutes | Cook Time: 15 minutes | Serves: 3

1 refrigerated piecrust (store-bought or see below)

1 pound McIntosh apples

2 tablespoons packed brown sugar

2 tablespoons dried cranberries

2 teaspoons all-purpose flour

½ teaspoon ground cinnamon

⅛ teaspoon grated nutmeg

¼ teaspoon grated orange rind

Pinch salt

1. Roll piecrust out on a floured surface. Cut out three (4½-inch) rounds with a glass and refrigerate on a baking sheet. 2. Peel, core, and cut apples into half-slices. 3. Toss apples, brown sugar, cranberries, flour, cinnamon, nutmeg, orange rind, and a pinch of salt in a microwave-safe bowl. Microwave on High for 2½ minutes or just until softened, stirring once. 4. Divide filling among 3 (6-ounce/3½-inch-diameter) ramekins. Place piecrust rounds on top, form a fluted edge, and cut a slit in the center. 5. Place the Crisper Tray in the bottom position. Place the ramekins on the tray and close the lid. Move SmartSwitch to AIR FRY/STOVETOP, and then use the center front arrows to select BAKE/ROAST. Set the cooking temperature to 350°F and the cooking time to 12 minutes. 6. Let the dish cool for 10 minutes and serve warm or at room temperature.

Per Serving: Calories 447; Fat: 19.26g; Sodium: 365mg; Carbs: 68.02g; Fiber: 4.9g; Sugar: 22.23g; Protein: 365g

Chocolate Croissants

Prep Time: 15 minutes | Cook Time: 10 minutes | Serves: 8

1 sheet frozen puff pastry, thawed

⅓ cup chocolate-hazelnut spread

1 large egg, beaten

1. On lightly floured surface, roll puff pastry into a 14-inch square. Cut pastry into quarters to form 4 squares. Cut each square diagonally to form 8 triangles. 2. Spread 2 teaspoons chocolate-hazelnut spread on each triangle; from wider end, roll up pastry. Brush egg on top of each roll. 3. Place the Crisper Tray in the bottom position. Add the rolls to it and close the lid. Move SmartSwitch to AIR FRY/STOVETOP, set the cooking temperature to 375°F and the cooking time to 8 minutes. 4. You can cook them in batches. 5. Let the dish cool for a while. Serve warm or at room temperature.

Per Serving: Calories 41; Fat: 2.83g; Sodium: 24mg; Carbs: 2.69g; Fiber: 0.1g; Sugar: 0.07g; Protein: 1.21g

Sweet 'n' Salty Granola Bark

Prep Time: 10 minutes | Cook Time: 16 minutes | Serves: 6

1 large egg white

⅓ cup maple syrup

1 teaspoon vanilla extract

¼ cup olive oil

¼ teaspoon salt

1½ cups old-fashioned oats

½ cup roasted, salted almonds, coarsely chopped

¼ cup sunflower seeds

¼ cup almond flour

¾ teaspoon ground cinnamon

Milk and fresh fruit (such as berries and peaches), for serving (optional)

1. Lightly beat egg white in a small bowl with a fork; measure out 1 tablespoon of the beaten egg white and set aside. Discard the remaining egg white or save for another use. 2. Cut a piece of parchment paper to line the bottom and halfway up the sides of the air fryer, pressing parchment against the sides and the bottom. 3. Combine maple syrup, vanilla, olive oil, salt, and 1 tablespoon beaten egg white in a clean bowl. 4. In a large bowl, combine oats, almonds, sunflower seeds, almond flour, and cinnamon. Add the maple syrup mixture to the dry ingredients and mix thoroughly. 5. Place the Crisper Tray in the bottom position. Evenly press half the mixture (1⅓ cups) into it and close the lid. Move SmartSwitch to AIR FRY/STOVETOP, set the cooking temperature to 325°F and the cooking time to 16 minutes. 6. Let it cool on the parchment on a wire rack for 1 hour before breaking it into chunks. 7. Do the same with the remaining oat mixture. 8. Serve the dish with milk and fruit, if desired. You can store the dish in an airtight container at room temperature for up to 7 days.

Per Serving: Calories 290; Fat: 17.34g; Sodium: 133mg; Carbs: 33.57g; Fiber: 6.8g; Sugar: 11.71g; Protein: 10.96g

Chocolate Molten Cakes

Prep Time: 20 minutes | Cook Time: 15 minutes | Serves: 4

¼ cup butter (½ stick), cut into pieces, plus more for greasing the custard cups

2 tablespoons granulated sugar, plus more for dusting

2 ounces semisweet chocolate, chopped

2 tablespoons heavy or whipping cream

¼ teaspoon vanilla extract

2 tablespoons all-purpose flour

1 large egg

1 large egg yolk

Confectioners' sugar, for dusting

Whipped cream or ice cream, for serving (optional)

1. Grease four 6-ounce custard cups; dust with granulated sugar. 2. Heat chocolate, butter, and cream in a saucepan over low heat until chocolate has melted and mixture is smooth, stirring occasionally. 3. Turn off the heat. Add vanilla and whisk in flour until mixture is smooth. 4. In a small bowl, with mixer at high speed, beat 2 tablespoons granulated sugar, whole egg, and egg yolk for 5 minutes until thick and pale yellow. Fold egg mixture, one-third at a time, into chocolate mixture until blended. 5. Divide batter evenly among prepared custard cups. 6. Place the Crisper Tray in the bottom position. Add the food to it and close the lid. Move SmartSwitch to AIR FRY/ STOVETOP, set the cooking temperature to 300°F and the cooking time to 10 minutes. 7. Cool on a wire rack for 5 minutes. Run a thin knife around the sides of the cups to loosen cakes; invert them onto plates. Dust with confectioners' sugar. 8. Serve immediately with whipped cream or ice cream, if desired.

Per Serving: Calories 231; Fat: 16.95g; Sodium: 126mg; Carbs: 16.7g; Fiber: 0.5g; Sugar: 11.29g; Protein: 3.41g

Stuffed Baked Apples

Prep Time: 5 minutes | Cook Time: 20 minutes | Serves: 4

4 to 6 tablespoons chopped walnuts

4 to 6 tablespoons raisins

4 tablespoons (½ stick) unsalted butter, melted

1 teaspoon ground cinnamon

½ teaspoon ground nutmeg

4 apples, cored but with the bottoms left intact

Vanilla ice cream, for topping

Maple syrup, for topping

1. Mix together the walnuts, raisins, melted butter, cinnamon, and nutmeg in a small bowl. 2. Scoop a quarter of the filling into each apple. 3. Place the apples in a suitable baking pan. 4. Place the Crisper Tray in the bottom position. Place the pan on the tray and close the lid. Move SmartSwitch to AIR FRY/STOVETOP, and then use the center front arrows to select BAKE/ROAST. Set the cooking temperature to 350°F and the cooking time to 20 minutes. 5. Serve the dish with vanilla ice cream and a drizzle of maple syrup.

Per Serving: Calories 221; Fat: 12.66g; Sodium: 7mg; Carbs: 25.35g; Fiber: 4.9g; Sugar: 18.26g; Protein: 2.83g

Coconut Toast

2 large eggs

¾ cup unsweetened coconut milk

2 tablespoons brown sugar

¼ teaspoon pumpkin pie spice

Pinch salt

4 (1-inch thick) slices brioche or Texas toast

1 cup crispy rice cereal

½ cup unsweetened, finely shredded coconut

Oil in mister

Mixed berries, confectioners' sugar, and maple syrup, for serving (optional)

1. In a shallow 1½-quart baking dish, whisk eggs, coconut milk, brown sugar, pumpkin pie spice, salt. Trim crusts off bread, if desired. 2. Place rice cereal in a shallow bowl and crush with a flat-bottomed dry measuring cup or a glass. Stir in coconut. 3. Dip bread in the egg mixture for about 10 seconds, coating both sides, then dip into the cereal-coconut mixture, again coating on both sides. Spray tops with oil. 4. Place the Crisper Tray in the bottom position. Add the bread to it with oil side down, and spray top with oil; close the lid. Move SmartSwitch to AIR FRY/STOVETOP, set the cooking temperature to 375°F and the cooking time to 8 minutes. 5. Transfer to a parchment-lined cookie sheet and keep warm in a 300°F oven. 6. Serve with mixed berries, confectioners' sugar, and maple syrup, if desired.

Per Serving: Calories 466; Fat: 32.9g; Sodium: 351mg; Carbs: 35.93g; Fiber: 4.2g; Sugar: 20.05g; Protein: 10.6g

Pecan-Stuffed Apples

4 Gala or Empire apples (about 1¼ pounds)

¼ cup chopped pecans

⅓ cup dried tart cherries

1 tablespoon melted butter

3 tablespoons brown sugar

¼ teaspoon allspice

Pinch salt

Ice cream, for serving

1. Cut off top ½ inch from each apple; reserve tops. Core through the stem ends without breaking through the bottom. 2. Combine pecans, cherries, butter, brown sugar, allspice, and a pinch of salt. Stuff the mixture into the hollow centers of the apples. Cover with apple tops. 3. Place the Crisper Tray in the bottom position. Add the food to it and close the lid. Move SmartSwitch to AIR FRY/STOVETOP, set the cooking temperature to 350°F and the cooking time to 25 minutes. 4. Serve the dish warm with ice cream.

Per Serving: Calories 197; Fat: 7.58g; Sodium: 65mg; Carbs: 32.27g; Fiber: 4.8g; Sugar: 25.48g; Protein: 1.19g

Homemade Pumpkin Fritters

Prep Time: 5 minutes | Cook Time: 10 minutes | Serves: 8

For Fritters

1 (16.3-ounce, 8-count) package refrigerated biscuit dough

½ cup chopped pecans

¼ cup pumpkin purée

¼ cup sugar

1 teaspoon pumpkin pie spice

2 tablespoons unsalted butter, melted

For Glaze

1 cup powdered sugar

1 teaspoon pumpkin pie spice

1 tablespoon pumpkin purée

2 tablespoons milk (plus more to thin the glaze, if necessary)

1. Turn the biscuit dough out onto a cutting board. 2. Cut each biscuit into 8 pieces. 3. Place them in a medium mixing bowl. Add the pecans, pumpkin, sugar, and pumpkin pie spice to the biscuit pieces and toss until well combined. 4. Shape the dough into 8 even mounds. 5. Drizzle butter over each of the fritters. 6. Place the Crisper Tray in the bottom position and spray it with olive oil. Add the food to it and close the lid. Move SmartSwitch to AIR FRY/STOVETOP, set the cooking temperature to 330°F and the cooking time to 7 minutes. 7. The dough should be cooked through and solid to the touch. If not, cook for 1 to 2 minutes more. 8. Gently remove the fritters from the air fryer. Let cool for about 10 minutes before you apply the glaze. 9. In a small mixing bowl, mix together the powdered sugar, pumpkin pie spice, pumpkin, and milk until smooth. 10. Drizzle the glaze over the fritters.

Per Serving: Calories 170; Fat: 9.41g; Sodium: 77mg; Carbs: 20.55g; Fiber: 1.1g; Sugar: 16.14g; Protein: 2.52g

Homemade Chocolate Chip Cookies

Prep Time: 5 minutes | Cook Time: 25 minutes | Serves: 5

1 cup (2 sticks) unsalted butter, at room temperature

1 cup granulated sugar

1 cup brown sugar

2 large eggs

½ teaspoon vanilla extract

1 teaspoon baking soda

½ teaspoon salt

3 cups all-purpose flour

2 cups chocolate chips

1. Cream the butter and both sugars in a large bowl. 2. Mix in the eggs, vanilla, baking soda, salt, and flour until well combined. Fold in the chocolate chips. 3. Knead the dough together, so everything is well mixed. 4. Spray a suitable baking sheet with cooking spray. 5. Using a cookie scoop or a tablespoon, drop heaping spoonfuls of dough onto the baking sheet about 1 inch apart. 6. Place the Crisper Tray in the bottom position. Place the molds on the tray and close the lid. Move SmartSwitch to AIR FRY/STOVETOP, and then use the center front arrows to select BAKE/ROAST. Set the cooking temperature to 340°F and the cooking time to 5 minutes. 7. When the cookies are golden brown and cooked through, use silicone oven mitts to remove the baking sheet from the air fryer and serve.

Per Serving: Calories 1017; Fat: 28.68g; Sodium: 618mg; Carbs: 175.46g; Fiber: 5.1g; Sugar: 99.03g; Protein: 14.26g

Apple Hand Pies

Prep Time: 5 minutes | Cook Time: 10 minutes | Serves: 8

1 package prepared pie dough

½ cup apple pie filling

1 large egg white

1 tablespoon Wilton White Sparkling Sugar

Caramel sauce, for drizzling

1. Lightly flour a clean work surface. Lay out the dough on the work surface. 2. Cut out 8 circles from the dough. 3. Gather up the scraps of dough, form them into a ball, and reroll them. 4. Cut out the remaining dough. 5. Add about 1 tablespoon of apple pie filling to the center of each circle. 6. Fold over the dough and use a fork to seal the edges. 7. Brush the egg white over the top, then sprinkle with sparkling sugar. 8. Place the Crisper Tray in the bottom position and spray it with olive oil. Place the pies on the tray and close the lid. Move SmartSwitch to AIR FRY/STOVETOP, and then use the center front arrows to select BAKE/ROAST. Set the cooking temperature to 350°F and the cooking time to 5 minutes. 9. Drizzle the dish with caramel sauce, if desired.

Per Serving: Calories 203; Fat: 11.16g; Sodium: 279mg; Carbs: 22.87g; Fiber: 0.1g; Sugar: 3.06g; Protein: 2.91g

Old-Fashioned Cherry Cobbler

Prep Time: 5 minutes | Cook Time: 35 minutes | Serves: 4

1 cup all-purpose flour

1 cup sugar

2 tablespoons baking powder

¾ cup milk

8 tablespoons (1 stick) unsalted butter

1 (21-ounce) can cherry pie filling

1. In a small mixing bowl, mix together the flour, sugar, and baking powder. Add the milk and mix until well blended. 2. Melt the butter in a small microwave-safe bowl in the microwave for about 45 seconds. 3. Pour the butter into the bottom of a suitable pan, then pour in the batter and spread it in an even layer. Pour the pie filing over the batter. Do not mix; the batter will bubble up through the filling during cooking. 4. Place the Crisper Tray in the bottom position. Place the pan on the tray and close the lid. Move SmartSwitch to AIR FRY/STOVETOP, and then use the center front arrows to select BAKE/ROAST. Set the cooking temperature to 320°F and the cooking time to 20 minutes. 5. When the cobbler is done the batter will be golden brown and cooked through. If not done, bake and recheck for doneness in 5-minute intervals. Overall cooking time will likely be between 30 and 35 minutes. 6. Let the dish cool slightly before serving.

Per Serving: Calories 557; Fat: 17.36g; Sodium: 64mg; Carbs: 96.17g; Fiber: 1.9g; Sugar: 26.85g; Protein: 6.15g

Chocolate-Frosted Doughnuts

Prep Time: 5 minutes | Cook Time: 5 minutes | Serves: 8

1 (16.3-ounce / 8-count) package refrigerated biscuit dough

¾ cup powdered sugar

¼ cup unsweetened cocoa powder

¼ cup milk

1. Unroll the biscuit dough onto a cutting board and separate the biscuits. 2. Cut out the center of each biscuit. 3. Place the Crisper Tray in the bottom position and spray it with oil. Add the doughnuts to it and close the lid. Move SmartSwitch to AIR FRY/STOVETOP, and then use the center front arrows to select BAKE/ROAST; set the cooking temperature to 330°F and the cooking time to 5 minutes. 4. Remove the doughnuts and let them cool slightly before glazing. 5. In a small mixing bowl, combine the powdered sugar, unsweetened cocoa powder, and milk and mix until smooth. 6. Dip the doughnuts into the glaze and use a knife to smooth the frosting evenly over the doughnut. 7. Let the glaze set before serving.

Per Serving: Calories 234; Fat: 7.08g; Sodium: 583mg; Carbs: 39.62g; Fiber: 2.4g; Sugar: 14.33g; Protein: 4.65g

Banana Cake

Prep Time: 5 minutes | Cook Time: 30 minutes | Serves: 4

⅓ cup brown sugar

4 tablespoons (½ stick) unsalted butter, at room temperature

1 ripe banana, mashed

1 large egg

2 tablespoons granulated sugar

1 cup all-purpose flour

1 teaspoon ground cinnamon

1 teaspoon vanilla extract

½ teaspoon ground nutmeg

1. Spray a suitable pan with cooking spray. 2. Cream the brown sugar and butter in a medium bowl until pale and fluffy. 3. Mix in the banana and egg. 4. Add the granulated sugar, flour, ground cinnamon, vanilla, and nutmeg and mix well. 5. Spoon the batter into the prepared pan. 6. Place the Crisper Tray in the bottom position. Place the molds on the tray and close the lid. Move SmartSwitch to AIR FRY/STOVETOP, and then use the center front arrows to select BAKE/ROAST. Set the cooking temperature to 320°F and the cooking time to 15 minutes. 7. Do a toothpick test. If the toothpick comes out clean, the cake is done. It there is batter on the toothpick, cook and check again in 5-minute intervals until the cake is done. It will likely take about 30 minutes total baking time to fully cook. 8. Set the pan on a wire cooling rack and let cool for about 10 minutes. Place a plate upside-down over the top of the pan. 9. Carefully flip the plate and the pan over, and set the plate on the counter. 10. Lift the pan off the cake. Frost as desired.

Per Serving: Calories 320; Fat: 9.56g; Sodium: 31mg; Carbs: 53.27g; Fiber: 2g; Sugar: 25.42g; Protein: 5.83g

Fried Plums

Prep Time: 5 minutes | Cook Time: 20 minutes | Serves: 6

6 plums cut into wedges

1 teaspoon ginger, ground

½ teaspoon cinnamon powder

Zest of 1 lemon, grated

2 tablespoons water

10 drops stevia

1. Combine the plums with the rest of the ingredients in a suitable pan. 2. Place the Crisper Tray in the bottom position. Place the molds on the tray and close the lid. Move SmartSwitch to AIR FRY/STOVETOP, and then use the center front arrows to select BAKE/ROAST. Set the cooking temperature to 360°F and the cooking time to 20 minutes. 3. Serve and enjoy.

Per Serving: Calories 44; Fat: 0.07g; Sodium: 9mg; Carbs: 11.48g; Fiber: 0.6g; Sugar: 10.47g; Protein: 0.21g

Chocolate Cake

Prep Time: 5 minutes | Cook Time: 30 minutes | Serves: 4

1¾ cups all-purpose flour

2 cups sugar

¾ cup unsweetened cocoa powder

1 teaspoon baking soda

1 teaspoon baking powder

½ cup vegetable oil

1 teaspoon salt

2 teaspoons vanilla extract

2 large eggs

1 cup milk

1 cup hot water

1. Spray a suitable baking pan with cooking spray. 2. In a large mixing bowl, combine the flour, sugar, cocoa powder, baking soda, baking powder, oil, salt, vanilla, eggs, milk, and hot water. 3. Pour the cake batter into the prepared pan. 4. Place the Crisper Tray in the bottom position. Place the pan on the tray and close the lid. Move SmartSwitch to AIR FRY/STOVETOP, and then use the center front arrows to select BAKE/ROAST. Set the cooking temperature to 330°F and the cooking time to 20 minutes. 5. Do a toothpick test. If the toothpick comes out clean, the cake is done. It there is batter on the toothpick, cook and check again in 5-minute intervals until the cake is done. It will likely take about 30 minutes total baking time to fully cook. 6. Set the pan on a wire cooling rack and let cool for about 10 minutes. Place a plate upside down over the top of the pan. 7. Carefully flip the plate and the pan over, and set the plate on the counter. Lift the pan off the cake.

Per Serving: Calories 744; Fat: 34.28g; Sodium: 965mg; Carbs: 104.98g; Fiber: 6.3g; Sugar: 52.78g; Protein: 13.63g

Fudge Brownies

Prep Time: 5 minutes | Cook Time: 20 minutes | Serves: 6

8 tablespoons (1 stick) unsalted butter, melted

1 cup sugar

1 teaspoon vanilla extract

2 large eggs

½ cup all-purpose flour

½ cup cocoa powder

1 teaspoon baking powder

1. Spray a suitable baking pan with cooking spray or grease the pan with butter. 2. In a medium mixing bowl, mix together the butter and sugar, then add the vanilla and eggs and beat until well combined. 3. Add the flour, cocoa powder, and baking powder and mix until smooth. 4. Pour the batter into the prepared pan. 5. Place the Crisper Tray in the bottom position. Place the pan on the tray and close the lid. Move SmartSwitch to AIR FRY/STOVETOP, and then use the center front arrows to select BAKE/ROAST. Set the cooking temperature to 350°F and the cooking time to 20 minutes. 6. Once the center is set, use silicon oven mitts to remove the pan. 7. Let the dish cool slightly before serving.

Per Serving: Calories 238; Fat: 12.92g; Sodium: 33mg; Carbs: 29.35g; Fiber: 2.4g; Sugar: 16.61g; Protein: 5.08g

Almond Cake with Chopped Plums

Prep Time: 10 minutes | Cook Time: 30 minutes | Serves: 8

½ cup butter, soft

3 eggs

½ cup swerve

¼ teaspoon almond extract

1 tablespoon vanilla extract

1½ cups almond flour

½ cup coconut flour

2 teaspoons baking powder

¾ cup almond milk

4 plums, pitted and chopped

1. Mix all the ingredients in a bowl. Pour the mixture into a cake pan lined with parchment paper. 2. Place the Crisper Tray in the bottom position. Place the pan on the tray and close the lid. Move SmartSwitch to AIR FRY/STOVETOP, and then use the center front arrows to select BAKE/ROAST. Set the cooking temperature to 370°F and the cooking time to 30 minutes. 3. Cool the cake down, slice and serve.

Per Serving: Calories 167; Fat: 13.55g; Sodium: 152mg; Carbs: 8.99g; Fiber: 0.5g; Sugar: 7.78g; Protein: 2.58g

Blueberry Pie

2 frozen pie crusts

2 (21-ounce) jars blueberry pie filling

1 teaspoon milk

1 teaspoon sugar

1. Remove the pie crusts from the freezer and let them thaw for 30 minutes on the countertop. 2. Place one crust into the bottom of a pie pan. 3. Pour the pie filling into the bottom crust, and then cover it with the other crust, being careful to press the bottom and top crusts together around the edge to form a seal. 4. Trim off any excess pie dough. 5. Cut venting holes in the top crust with a knife or a small decoratively shaped cookie cutter. 6. Brush the top crust with milk, then sprinkle the sugar over it. 7. Place the Crisper Tray in the bottom position. Place the pie on the tray and close the lid. Move SmartSwitch to AIR FRY/STOVETOP, and then use the center front arrows to select BAKE/ ROAST. Set the cooking temperature to 310°F and the cooking time to 15 minutes. If it needs additional time, reset the timer and bake for an additional 3 minutes. 8. Let the dish cool for 15 minutes before serving.

Per Serving: Calories 398; Fat: 2.28g; Sodium: 285mg; Carbs: 65.37g; Fiber: 3g; Sugar: 37.91g; Protein: 2.28g

Cream Muffins

Prep Time: 15 minutes | Cook Time: 15 minutes | Serves: 4

4 teaspoons cream cheese

1 egg, beaten

½ teaspoon baking powder

1 teaspoon vanilla extract

4 teaspoons almond flour

4 teaspoons coconut flour

2 tablespoons heavy cream

2 teaspoons Erythritol

Cooking spray

1. Mix up cream cheese, egg, baking powder, vanilla extract, almond flour, coconut flour, heavy cream, and Erythritol. 2. Spray the air fryer muffin molds with cooking spray. Pour the batter in the muffin molds (fill ½ part of every mold). 3. Place the Crisper Tray in the bottom position. Place the molds on the tray and close the lid. Move SmartSwitch to AIR FRY/STOVETOP, and then use the center front arrows to select BAKE/ROAST. Set the cooking temperature to 365°F and the cooking time to 11 minutes. 4. Cool the cooked muffins and remove them from the molds.

Per Serving: Calories 68; Fat: 5.86g; Sodium: 46mg; Carbs: 1.33g; Fiber: 0.2g; Sugar: 0.74g; Protein: 2.18g

Conclusion

Are you seeking to begin your weight loss journey and embrace a healthier way of life? The Ninja Speedi is the perfect choice for you! This versatile 12-in-1 kitchen appliance can air fry, crisp, roast, bake, broil, reheat, and dehydrate meats and vegetables, making it the perfect choice for whipping up healthier desserts and snacks. With its advanced technology, this all-in-one appliance removes excess fats from your food while still achieving the desired level of crispiness. Plus, its high-capacity pot and dishwasher-safe accessories make it easy to cook for the whole family. And if you need some inspiration, the included cookbook offers plenty of delicious and nutritious meal ideas. Start your journey to a healthier lifestyle today with the Ninja Speedi!

Appendix 1 Measurement Conversion Chart

VOLUME EQUIVALENTS (LIQUID)

US STANDARD	US STANDARD (OUNCES)	METRIC (APPROXIMATE)
2 tablespoons	1 fl.oz	30 mL
¼ cup	2 fl.oz	60 mL
½ cup	4 fl.oz	120 mL
1 cup	8 fl.oz	240 mL
1½ cup	12 fl.oz	355 mL
2 cups or 1 pint	16 fl.oz	475 mL
4 cups or 1 quart	32 fl.oz	1 L
1 gallon	128 fl.oz	4 L

VOLUME EQUIVALENTS (DRY)

US STANDARD	METRIC (APPROXIMATE)
⅛ teaspoon	0.5 mL
¼ teaspoon	1 mL
½ teaspoon	2 mL
¾ teaspoon	4 mL
1 teaspoon	5 mL
1 tablespoon	15 mL
¼ cup	59 mL
½ cup	118 mL
¾ cup	177 mL
1 cup	235 mL
2 cups	475 mL
3 cups	700 mL
4 cups	1 L

TEMPERATURES EQUIVALENTS

FAHRENHEIT(F)	CELSIUS (C) (APPROXIMATE)
225 ℉	107 ℃
250 ℉	120 ℃
275 ℉	135 ℃
300 ℉	150 ℃
325 ℉	160 ℃
350 ℉	180 ℃
375 ℉	190 ℃
400 ℉	205 ℃
425 ℉	220 ℃
450 ℉	235 ℃
475 ℉	245 ℃
500 ℉	260 ℃

WEIGHT EQUIVALENTS

US STANDARD	METRIC (APPROXINATE)
1 ounce	28 g
2 ounces	57 g
5 ounces	142 g
10 ounces	284 g
15 ounces	425 g
16 ounces (1 pound)	455 g
1.5 pounds	680 g
2 pounds	907 g

Appendix 2 Recipes Index

Made in the USA
Las Vegas, NV
11 December 2024

13890125R00065